Essential
Cyprus

by Robert Bulmer

Robert Bulmer lived for many years in Cyprus.
He returns often, to walk in the hills, explore
again the towns and villages or simply luxuriate
on the beaches. His book *Days Out in Cyprus*,
published by himself, was followed by the AA's
first edition of *Essential Cyprus* and then by
AA Thomas Cook *Travellers Cyprus*.

AA Publishing

Page 1: *Kyrenia harbour*

Page 5a: *Temple of Apollo, Kourion*
5b: *Wedding party at Agía Napa*

Page15a: *Frescoes at Kykkos Monastery*
15b: *Aphrodite of Soli, Cyprus Museum, Nicosia*

Page 27a: *Chapel alongside Stavrovouni Monastery*
27b: *Nissi Beach sails*

Page 91a: *Ágios Irakleidios fresco*
91b: *Greek Orthodox monk at Agía Ekaterina*

Page 117a: *Limassol Beach*
117b: *Bust of Athenian Kimon at Larnaka*

Find out more about AA Publishing and the wide range of services the AA provides by visiting our Web site at www.theaa.co.uk.

Written by Robert Bulmer

Edited, designed and produced by AA Publishing.
© The Automobile Association 1998
Maps © The Automobile Association 1998

Distributed in the United Kingdom by AA Publishing, Norfolk House, Priestley Road, Basingstoke, Hampshire, RG24 9NY.

A CIP catalogue record for this book is available from the British Library.

ISBN 0 7495 1618 6

Published by AA Publishing, a trading name of Automobile Association Developments Limited, whose registered office is Norfolk House, Priestley Road, Basingstoke, Hampshire, RG24 9NY.
Registered number 1878835.

Colour separation: BTB Digital Imaging, Whitchurch, Hampshire

Printed and bound in Italy by Printer Trento srl

Contents

About this Book

KEY TO SYMBOLS

🗺 map reference to the maps found in the What to See section (see below)

✉ address or location

☎ telephone number

🕐 opening times

🍴 restaurant or café on premises or near by

Ⓜ nearest underground train station

🚌 nearest bus/tram route

🚆 nearest overground train station

🚢 ferry crossings and excursions by boat

✈ travel by air

ℹ tourist information

♿ facilities for visitors with disabilities

✋ admission charge

↔ other places of interest near by

❓ other practical information

▶ indicates the page where you will find a fuller description

---

Essential *Cyprus* is divided into five sections to cover the most important aspects of your visit to Cyprus.

Viewing Cyprus pages 5–14
An introduction to Cyprus by the author
Cyprus's Features
Essence of Cyrpus
The Shaping of Cyprus
Peace and Quiet
Cyprus's Famous

Top Ten pages 15–26
The author's choice of the Top Ten places to visit in Cyprus, each with practical information

What to See pages 27–90
The five main areas of Cyprus, each with its own brief introduction and an alphabetical listing of the main attractions
Practical information
Snippets of 'Did You Know...' information
5 suggested walks
5 suggested drives
2 features

Where To... pages 91–116
Detailed listings of the best places to eat, stay, shop, take the children and be entertained

4

Practical Matters pages 117–24
A highly visual section containing essential travel information

Maps
All map references are to the individual maps found in the What to See section of this guide.
For example, Kourion has the reference 🗺 28B1 – indicating the page on which the map is located and the grid square in which the site is to be found. A list of the maps that have been used in this travel guide can be found in the index.

Prices
Where appropriate, an indication of the cost of an establishment is given by £ signs: £££ denotes higher prices, ££ denotes average prices, while £ denotes lower charges.

Star Ratings
Most of the places described in this book have been given a separate rating:

✪✪✪ Do not miss
✪✪ Highly recommended
✪ Worth seeing

Viewing
Cyprus

5

Robert Bulmer's Cyprus

Climate Extremes

Cyprus in summer is a hot place, certainly the hottest of the Mediterranean islands, and, of course, sun worshippers love it. It is difficult to imagine that winter days can be cool and wet with vast amounts of snow falling on the highest ground, creating a winter wonderland among the pine trees.

Cyprus, within sight of Asia Minor, is halfway to the Orient. Yet it looks westwards, attracting many visitors from Europe and aspiring to membership of the EU. A legacy of British Colonial rule is excellent English that is spoken island wide. Western ideas are very well received. Nevertheless, Cyprus remains different and retains its own culture. This is a complex mixture stemming from its location and history. Over the centuries Cyprus has been controlled by most Mediterranean powers and the people have a diverse, if not exotic, ancestry.

The separation of the island today is an indirect consequence of the arrival of the Ottoman Turks in the 16th century. It is not a division easily ignored – United Nations soldiers and Greek and Turkish flags are everywhere along the Green Line. Nevertheless few visitors dwell on the political situation. Understandably they have other distractions.

In the south there are 340km of coast to explore, along with the fascinating Troodos massif and the towns of Larnaka, Limassol, Pafos and Nicosia. Visitors in the north have to be content with long unspoilt shores, including the fabled Karpasia peninsula and the magnificent Kyrenian Hills. The remarkable Mesaoria is there for good measure.

Where the friendliness of the people comes from is something of a mystery. Middle Eastern tradition demands hospitality for travellers, but in Cyprus it goes further – guests can be fed to bursting and an enduring memory for many visitors is the simple generosity of the islanders.

In Cyprus the oranges come straight from the tree

Cyprus's Features

Geography

- The island has two significant mountain ranges. Troodos in the centre reaches 1,951m, high enough to ensure snow cover in winter; the Kyrenia range, at 1,046m, is now in the Turkish controlled sector of the island.
- There are approximately 3,350 hours of sunshine a year, with little chance of rain between May and October.
- The sheep cope with the shortage of grazing in the dry summer by storing fat in their tails.

Population

- The first sign of human habitation dates from 9,000 years ago.
- The island's population is 725,000, of whom about 576,000 are Greek Cypriots and 134,000 Turkish Cypriots, about 18 per cent of the total.
- The dowry system was made illegal in 1994.

Economic Factors

- Forty six per cent of the land area is cultivated, the main crops being cereals, potatoes and citrus fruits.
- Cyprus has the third highest standard of living in the Mediterranean. The average income here is twice as high as it is in Greece.
- A dam building programme has increased capacity from 6 million cu m in 1961 to 300 million in 1991. A desalination plant which has been built at Dhekalia provides 20,000cu m a day.

Tourism

- The island attracts over 2 million visitors a year and tourism provides employment for some 35,000 people or 13 per cent of the workforce.

It is a hard life for sheep in summer; these are hoping for grazing in the Avgas Gorge

Essence of Cyprus

The coffee shop, a male preserve, does not have the history of a Roman column, but it has a remarkable capacity to resist change

Cyprus is a land of contour and light, hills, valleys and plains. Beaches there are, although not endless sands along the shore. The heat of summer robs the land of life; winter rains restore spectacular colour. With its archaeological wonders Cyprus is certainly the stuff of tourist literature.

But what of the less tangible Cyprus? There is the interesting first journey to the hotel with squealing brakes and tyres; less disconcerting are the marvellous alfresco gastronomic events under awnings at lunch time and the stars at night. Walks through the pine forests of the high mountains will long be remembered, as will the friendliness of the people.

THE 10 ESSENTIALS

If you only have a short time to visit Cyprus, or would like to get a really complete picture of the island, here are the essentials:

Armada of pedalos off Agia Napa

• **Go to the Roman theatre at Kourion** (► 18–19) for a classical drama: the atmosphere is electric. They are held regularly throughout the summer, details from the tourist office.

• **Find a quiet beach**, preferably fringed with bushes or tall grasses, and take a swim long before breakfast.

• **Have a drink in a village coffee shop**. Be prepared to be ignored, but it is much more likely that someone will chance their English and start a conversation.

• **Have a full *meze* alfresco style off the tourist track**. Be prepared to stay awake all night with a distended stomach.

• **Drive to Petra tou Romiou**, or Rock of Romios (► 50) in the late afternoon and stop on the cliff top a little to the east. The view is tremendous.

• **Join in a Greek dance**. The impressiveness of the steps is hardly matched by the difficulty. Take a couple of brandy sours first.

• **Join a plate-breaking session in a Greek tavern**. This mayhem is not as common as it once was, but local enquiries may lead to a venue.

• **Get invited to a village wedding**, witness the chaotic church service and drink and eat all night under the stars.

• **Ski or toboggan on Mount Olympus**. No chance here for summer visitors, the season is from 1st January to the end of March.

• **Walk a forest trail in the Troodos or Kyrenia Mountains** until perspiring freely, then sit down and have a picnic.

Kourion Theatre, once a place for spectacular Roman gladitorial contests, hosts a Greek wedding

The Shaping of Cyprus

9000–3800 BC
First immigrants from Asia Minor. Neolithic settlements built at Khirokitia, Cape Andreas.

3800–2500 BC
Chalcolithic period. Erimi and Lemba became important centres of habitation.

2500–1050 BC
Bronze Age. Settlers arrive from all parts of the eastern Mediterranean. Alambra and Nitovikla the principal locations.

1050–750 BC
Transition to Iron Age.

700 BC
Assyrian rule.

570 BC
Egyptian King Amasis becomes effective ruler of Cyprus.

545 BC
Cyprus submits voluntarily to King Cyrus of Persia. Two hundred years of slavery follow.

325–50 BC
Cyprus becomes part of the Greek world. The people adopt Greek dress and Greek architectural styles are imitated.

50 BC–AD 330
Roman occupation and the building of great amphitheatres, baths and temples.

AD 45
Visit of St Paul.

King Cyrus of Persia (550–529 BC)

330–1191
Split in Roman Empire and the start of the Byzantine era. Seventh- and 10th-century Arab raids.

1191
Richard the Lionheart arrives, en route to Syria, during the third Crusade, and marries Princess Berengaria in Limassol.

1192–1489
Lusignan Rule. The great Latin cathedrals of Nicosia and Famagusta are built.

1489–1571
Venetian forces, invited to help against troublesome Genoese contingent in Famagusta, take island for themselves.

1571–1878
Ottoman Turks realise long held ambitions to subjugate Cyprus.

1878
Britain, in agreement with Turkey, takes control of the island to foil Russian encroachment.

1914
Cyprus formally annexed by Britain as a consequence of Turkey fighting for Germany in World War I.

1955
Terrorist campaign by EOKA (Ethniki Organosis Kyprion Agoniston, or the National Organis- ation of Cypriot

The Queen inspects a guard of honour on her arrival at RAF Akrotiri

Fighters), under Grivas, commences. Their mission to wage guerrilla war against the British.

1960
Cyprus granted Independence. Archbishop Makarios III becomes president.

1963
Inter-communal fighting. Turks retreat into enclaves.

1964
United Nations soldiers sent to keep the peace.

1974
Military coup against Makarios, who flees the island. Five days later Turkish forces invade and soon take control of north Cyprus. Rauf Denktash appointed leader. Makarios returns to south Cyprus.

1975
As Nicosia airport remains in United Nations control, Greek Cypriots build airport at Larnaka and revive tourist industry with massive hotel building programme.

1977
Makarios dies and is succeeded by President Kyprianou.

1983
Turks unilaterally proclaim Republic of Northern Cyprus.

1984
United Nations sponsored talks end in a stalemate.

1993
Queen Elizabeth II visits the island and attends Commonwealth Heads of Government Conference.

1996
Trouble flares on the Green Line, Nicosia's buffer zone, resulting in the deaths of two Greek Cypriots.

11

Peace & Quiet

Akamas's Gorges

A few companies, including Exalt Travel of Pafos (☎ 06 243803) offer guided tours through the gorges, the Avgas being the favourite. It is something of an adventure, negotiating the boulder strewn river bed with high sheer cliffs on either side. If the weather is, or is likely to be bad, the gorges should be avoided – flash floods here are extremely dangerous.

Cedar Valley

This is best reached from Pafos, Pano Panagia (► 67) being the last outpost before setting out on the unmetalled track into the western forest. The valley is perhaps 12km away, a good map is needed and a jeep is the best vehicle for the uncertainties ahead.

At 400m above sea level, under the canopy of trees, the air is cool. The cedars are magnificent specimens and the stillness of the forest is only likely to be disturbed by the crashing of a moufflon taking fright, or the trickle of water from a perennial spring.

Western forest en route to the fabled cedars

Diarizos River

Park the car where the Pafos–Limassol road crosses the river. The turning to Palaia Pafos (► 63) is a little further east; the turning to distant Platres about 1km to the west. The stone arched pedestrian bridge is a good landmark. A track on the west bank leads, in about 2km, to the sea.

Grasses and reeds line the banks and there is a good chance of spotting the purple heron and other interesting water birds. In the dry summer months, the river is reduced to a trickle.

Famagusta Bay

The stretch of coast starting about 9km north of Protaras, offers some fine cliff-top walks. Access is not entirely obvious. Once on the low escarpments all is straightforward, a bonus being the view of the forbidden city of Famagusta (► 83) – take binoculars.

Karpasia

Much of northern Cyprus is quiet, but the Karpasia is even quieter, with only the local population going about their business. Visitors should take a map and simply set off on a journey of exploration stopping at any beach, ancient site or village that attracts their attention.

Petounda Point

Take the road west of Kition village towards Petounda Point for about 10km. Keep parallel to the shore until it closes on the road. After another 300–400m it is time to abandon the car, find the pebbly shore and have a picnic. It is unlikely that anyone else will be there.

Pomos Point to Kato Pyrgos

This section of coast sees fewer visitors than most others in southern Cyprus, although nothing is guaranteed. Several stretches of dark sand line the varied bays and coves. The further east the quieter it is. Here the Troodos Mountains descend dramatically to the sea. In the event of a sudden influx of tourist buses there is the opportunity to retreat quickly into the quiet hills and gaze down on the coast from a good height.

The secluded beaches near Pomos Point face north but are no less splendid for that

Timi Beach

Timi Beach is not the best of Cyprus's watering places, but the series of sandy coves with the occasional fisherman's boat have a certain charm. The sea is generally calm and it is quiet except at weekends when the locals descend upon it from nearby villages.

Cyprus's Famous

Visitors to Cyprus
Few native Cypriots have achieved international celebrity but the island has attracted illustrious visitors throughout its history. Island mythology claims the birth of Aphrodite and visits from a succession of Greek gods. Christian influences were brought by St Paul, St Barnabas and St Lazarus and literary visitors have included, Rimbaud, Lawrence Durrell and Colin Thubron. More recently, as a sign of its status as a world troublespot, a succession of international statesmen have been despatched here in attempts to solve the 'Cyprus Problem'.

Makarios

Archbishop Makarios was the first President of Cyprus. He remains a great national hero and statues of him can be seen all around the island.

He was born in 1913 and became a priest at Kykkos Monastery. After a period working in Greece and the United States, he was appointed Bishop of Pafos and later Archbishop of the whole island. He soon became part of the highly politicised world of the Cypriot Church and their campaign for Enosis, or Union, with Greece and against the British. In 1956, as a result of these activities, he was deported to the Seychelles. A year later he was freed but was not allowed to return to Cyprus. It was from Athens, therefore, that he began the final negotiations for independence, having abandoned Enosis, and in February 1959 a deal was signed. Independence was formally granted in August 1960.

Makarios then became President, but inter-communal strife soon emerged and the United Nations had to keep the peace. Tensions continued to grow and in 1974 Makarios was deposed in a military coup led by some remnants of the EOKA movement, who were still campaigning for union with Greece. Makarios escaped, but Turkey invaded and the island was divided, as it remains today. He returned and ruled for another three years before his death in 1977, ushering in a new secular era in Cypriot politics.

Richard the Lionheart

Richard I of England came to Cyprus on his way to the Crusades and changed the course of the island's history. Part of his fleet was shipwrecked in 1191, including his sister and his fiancée, Berengaria. The ruler of Cyprus, Isaac Comnenos, treated them badly and Richard retaliated militarily, having first married Berengaria in St George's Chapel, Limassol. After a month of battles Comnenos surrendered and Richard took control of the whole island. However, he was not much enamoured with his conquest and, fearing it would be more trouble than it was worth, arranged to pass it on to Guy de Lusignan, a French knight. This ushered in a 300-year rule by the Lusignan dynasty.

Archbishop Makarios, the island's first President and a national hero

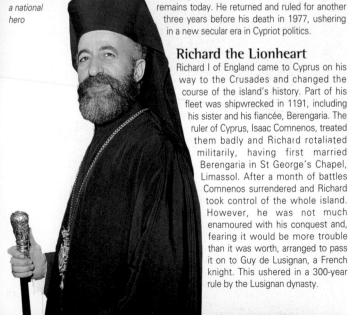

Top Ten

1

Akamas

✚ 28A2

✉ Cyprus's westernmost land

🍴 Baths of Aphrodite Tourist Pavilion Café (££)

❓ Across the road from the café is a pool under the trees called The Baths of Aphrodite

A beautiful region of hills, valleys and rocky shores, ideal for rambling, with rich and varied flora and diverse wildlife habitats.

This westernmost extremity of Cyprus is unique in the Greek part of the island, not only for its beauty but also for the absence of tourist development. This can be explained partly by its remoteness, but more so by the existence of a firing range of the British Forces – a rich irony.

The vegetation is Mediterranean, with large tracts of impenetrable maquis interspersed with a thin covering of pine trees and juniper. Autumn flowering cyclamen is everywhere. In places the landscape is impressively stark with spectacular rock outcrops. On the beaches green and loggerhead turtles still come up to lay their eggs, and occasionally a monk seal may be sighted.

Although there are no metal roads, the area is becoming rather popular, especially with motorcyclists.

Several trails for ramblers have been created, starting by the Baths of Aphrodite, west of Polis. A network of marked paths traverse the hills and inform the walker of the types of flora. These are described in a free booklet from the tourist office called *Nature Trails of the Akamas*. The ascent of Mouti tis Sotiras is worth contemplating, it only takes an hour to reach the summit and the view is surely the best in Greek Cyprus. Needless to say, in summer it is a hot and sticky expedition. An alternative is to take a boat from Latsi for a swim and a picnic in one of the delightful coves, perhaps near Fontana Amoroza (Love's Spring), halfway to Cape Arnaoutis.

The magnificent and unspoilt Akamas coast

2
Hala Sultan Tekke & Salt Lake

A Muslim holy shrine standing on the shore of a natural landmark which has very different aspects in winter and summer.

🕇 29D2

✉ 3km west of Larnaka on the Kition road

🕐 Jun–Sep, daily 7:30–7:30; Oct–May, daily 7:30–5

The Hala Sultan Tekke's importance is surpassed only by the shrines of Mecca, Medina and al Aksha (Jerusalem). It was here that the prophet Mohammed's maternal aunt, Umm Haram, was buried in AD 649. Apparently, she fell from a donkey and broke her neck whilst participating in an Arab raid on the island. Three enormous stones were raised to mark her grave and thereafter the site became an important place of pilgrimage for Muslims.

The mosque, with its distinctive dome and minaret, was built by the Turks in 1816, although the tomb was built in 1760. Visitors are permitted to enter the mosque but must respect the dress code and remove their shoes before entering.

In the summer the surrounding gardens with their impressive palm trees are a relatively cool haven from the blistering heat of the Salt Lake. This is a desert for much of the year, but in winter the lake fills with water and attracts a wide range of migrating birds.

The most spectacular of the winter visitors are the flamingoes, whose distinctive pink colour makes an attractive sight. In summer the water evaporates, leaving a dusty grey expanse which shimmers in the heat.

The salt used to be a significant product in the island's economy, but today it is no longer economically viable to collect it. It originates from the nearby sea, seeping up through the porous rocks during the rainy months.

🚌 Bus from Larnaka centre with drop-off on the main road

✋ Free, but donation requested

↔ Kition (Panagia Angeloktistos) (➤ 40)

3
Kourion

28B1

Off the Limassol to Pafos road

Jun–Sep, daily 7:30–7:30; Oct–May 7:30–5. Visitors should also note that excavations are still in progress on the site and this can mean that some parts are closed at times

Café in the tourist pavilion (£)

From Limassol and Pafos

Cheap

Kolossi (▶ 48), Temple of Apollo Hylates (▶ 50)

Classical dramas or productions of Shakespeare are performed throughout the summer. The tourist office will have the programme

Kourion is the most important archaeological site in the Greek part of the island, impressively perched on the cliffs overlooking the sea.

There has been some sort of settlement here since 3300 BC, the very early Neolithic period, but the first significant town was probably built by the Mycenaeans around 1400 BC. It reached the height of its powers under the Romans and it is that influence which is the most evident from the ruins. Thereafter it went into decline as it suffered from the attentions of Arab raiders and the population moved inland. Excavations started in 1873 and have continued ever since.

The Theatre presents the most striking image of the whole site. It seated an audience of 3,500 and was probably built by the early Greeks and then extended by the Romans to allow for gladiatorial combat and for man against animal spectacles. It is entirely restored and, in summer, performances of plays and concerts are staged.

The Annexe of Eustolios lies just uphill from the Theatre and has an impressive mosaic floor which can be observed from raised gangways which run around the courtyard. Further up the hill are the Baths which also had mosaic floors. The Baths follow the traditional Roman pattern, with the Frigidarium (cold room), then the Tepidarium (warm room) and the Caldarium (hot baths). Various mechanisms

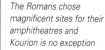

for heating the water, along with furnaces and water tanks, are still in evidence.

At the top of the hill west of the Theatre is the Building of the Achilles Mosaic. Constructed around a courtyard, it has a mosaic showing Achilles in disguise revealing his true identity to Odysseus by mistake. There is also a depiction of Ganymede and the Eagle. The house dates from about AD 4 and was probably a reception area for visitors. A similar house lies a short distance down the track, where the mosaic shows two gladiators in combat. Also visible are the remains of an aqueduct which brought the settlement's water supply to the Fountain House, traces of which can still be seen. Opposite the Fountain House is the Basilica which was built in the 5th century. It has fragments of mosaic still visible on the floor and was once supported on 12 columns, some of which can still be detected.

This site covers the main areas of interest, but about 1km towards Pafos off the main road is the Stadium which once had seating for 6,000. The site is openly accessible and the shape of the arena can be made out, as can some of the seats.

The Romans chose magnificent sites for their amphitheatres and Kourion is no exception

4
Kykkos Monastery

✝ 28B2

✉ West of Pedoulas, western Troodos

🕐 Daily

🍴 Café near by (£)

✋ Free; museum cheap

A solemn-faced depiction of the Madonna at Kykkos

The monastery is the largest and richest foundation in Cyprus and is known throughout the orthodox world.

Kykkos is sited high and alone in the hills of western Cyprus, but even at 1,318m above sea level it is overlooked by higher ground. In summer its cloisters and courtyards are cool; in winter when the mist descends, the temperature drops alarmingly. Cypriots make pilgrimages to Kykkos from all over southern Cyprus, and hundreds may visit in a weekend. These numbers are swollen by sightseeing tourists from the holiday centres.

Kykkos was built about 900 years ago for its icon, the painting of which is attributed to St Luke and was given to a Cypriot monk by the Emperor Comnenos for relieving his daughter's sciatica. The present construction with two main courtyards is not of great antiquity – fires destroyed earlier buildings and nothing is older than the 19th century.

In contrast with the spartan conditions of earlier times, today's monks have many of the modern comforts of life. Even so, over the years, the community has dwindled from hundreds to a handful and even fewer novices.

The famous icon is called Elousa. It has been encased in silver for 200 years and anyone attempting to gaze directly on it does so under sufferance of horrible punishment. Photography is not permitted. There is also a small one-room museum with items of interest from the monastery's past, mainly religious regalia and books.

In 1926 a novice called Michael Mouskos came to the monastery. He was to become Archbishop Makarios III, and President of Cyprus. In those days he would be awake for prayers at 5:30AM followed by a frugal breakfast. During the later EOKA campaign the monastery was used by the guerillas for communications and the handling of supplies.

Makarios is buried on the hill called Throni, situated directly above the monastery.

5
Lara

A remote and beautiful area where the land sweeps up to the high hills and turtles come ashore to breed.

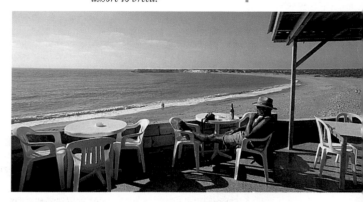

Lara is the name of a headland with sandy bays on each side. This splendid coast continues on up to Koppos Island where the rough road gives out, and then on to the distant north cape.

The nearest outpost is Agios Georgios, hardly a village but having a church and harbour and, of course, a restaurant. It sees the last of the hard surface road, and from now on the track is terrible, best attempted with a jeep-type vehicle or a motorcycle. And there is quite a lot of it – 8km in all, with one steep area that is a real test of nerve on the cliff edge. Thicket, thorn and mimosa border the road, and only by chance or local knowledge can sandy coves on the rocky shore be found. The beaches of Lara itself are easier to discover, with a sweeping bay to the north and a smaller one to the south.

Lara is now a popular destination for there are regular boat trips from Pafos calling at Agios Georgios on the way. Such splendid beaches and scenery would attract visitors in any circumstances, but there is further incentive – Lara's famous turtles. In an attempt to secure the future of these beleaguered and precious amphibians a hatchery has been established at Lara. Paradoxically, this was accompanied by great publicity and many make the trip in the hope of seeing them; in fact there is no certainty of this, much depends on the cycle of the breeding season. An even greater paradox is the proposal to create a holiday resort at Lara by the diocese of Pafos, an intrusion which can only detract from the magnificence of the area.

Looking north to Lara headland and the site of the turtle hatchery

 28A2

 Western Cyprus, north of Pafos

 Café near the headland (£)

 Free

21

6
Mosaics at Pafos

28A2

✉ Inland from the harbour

☎ 06 240217

🌐 Mon–Fri 7:30–5,
Sat–Sun 9–5. Closed
1 Jan, 25 Dec, Greek
Orthodox Easter Sun

🍴 Cafés at the harbour (££)

✋ Moderate

↔ Saranda Kolones (➤ 60),
St Paul's Pillar (➤ 60),
Pafos Fort (➤ 59)

Roman houses with very impressive and well preserved mosaics depicting colourful scenes from Greek mythology.

The mosaics were found in five large 3rd-century villas which probably belonged to wealthy Roman noblemen. The House of Dionysos was the first to be excavated, after a passing shepherd turned up some fragments of mosaics. The depictions include that of Ganymede being taken to Olympus by an eagle. The most famous mosaic is that of the triumph of Dionysos as he heads across the skies in a chariot drawn by leopards. According to the legend, Dionysos was the first person to discover how to make wine, and his followers are depicted enjoying the fruits of his labour.

The House of Aion displays a very fine series of mosaics which were discovered in 1983. The five scenes starting from the top left show Leda and the Swan; the baby Dionysos; then the middle panel depicts a beauty contest being judged by Aion; on the bottom row is the triumphant procession of Dionysos and the punishment of a musician, Marsyas, who had challenged Apollo to a musical contest and lost. These mosiacs date from the late 4th century.

The House of Orpheus contains representations of Amazon, Hercules and the Lion of Nemea, alongside a very impressive

The Roman mosaics display great variety in colour and pattern

mosaic featuring Orpheus surrounded by animals who are listening to his music.

The main mosaic in the House of Theseus is that of Theseus killing the minotaur, although there are some others featuring Achilles and Neptune. The mosaics here are less well preserved than in other areas of the site. A new area – the House of the Four Seasons – was unearthed in 1992. Mosaics showing the Gods of the Seasons and a variety of hunting scenes were found here. As excavations are continuing, parts of these houses may not be open to the public.

7
Nicosia Walled City

Eleven stout bastions superimposed on a circular plan give the city its distinctive and unique form. Much has survived the centuries.

28C3

Centre of Nicosia

Cafés at Laïki Geitonia, Famagusta Gate, Attatürk Square (£)

Nicosia (► 70)

Nicosia's formidable ramparts, so masterfully constructed by the Venetians, remain substantially intact, although Pafos Gate to the west is battered and Girne (Kyrenia) Kapisi's situation ruined. Famagusta Gate has fared better, although it is now a cultural centre, perhaps something of a comedown for what was the important eastern entrance into the city. A lesser but similar indignity has been inflicted on the wide moat (always intended to be dry), this deep and formidable barrier to full scale attack is now a collection of very pleasant gardens, car parks and football pitches. In the end the great walls did not save Nicosia, the Turks broke through in 1570 after a siege of 70 days – a bloody event, with the victors celebrating in an orgy of slaughter.

Today Ledra and Onasagoras Streets in the Greek sector are thriving bustling places, and the small shops of

Traffic negotiating streets originally designed for the donkey cart

all kinds are continuously busy. A little to the east the reconstructed buildings known as Laïki Geitonia (► 74) are popular with visitors. In the Turkish part of town development moves at a somewhat slower pace.

Along the backstreets there are areas which are conspicuously decrepit. This is not always to be regretted, as low overheads have enabled a Bohemian quarter to grow up around Famagusta Gate, with bars, cafés, a bookshop or two and a small theatre. Close by is a renovated neighbourhood. The buildings, mainly houses, remain substantially as before, but wearing new clothes. Small interesting squares, once rough underfoot, are now smoothly paved.

Of course, Nicosia is the city of the Green Line, a barrier of sandbags and barbed wire which was erected before the young conscripts who now guard it were born.

8
St Hilarion Castle

28C3

✉ High in the hills west of Kyrenia

🕐 Daily 8:30–5

🍴 Café at the gate (£)

✋ Cheap

↔ Bellapais Abbey (▶ 88)

This fortified former monastery, besieged then taken by Richard the Lionheart in 1191, has spectacular coastal views.

Richard the Lionheart laid siege to the castle in 1191, and after four days emperor Isaac Comnenos surrendered. Today the Turkish military controls the heights around the castle, and it is a significant place to advertise their presence.

This is no compact, easily visited site. There are lower, middle and upper wards, with quite a distance between each and a steep climb to the upper section. The big compensation for the effort – reasonably substantial in the summer heat – is the unbelievable view. The north shore is directly below and Turkey is plainly visible in the clear air of the cooler months. East and west a spectacular line of peaks and ridges run into the distance.

St Hilarion, it seems, was a recluse who found refuge on these heights, and built a retreat here. A monastery was established on the site in the 11th century, and was later fortified and then extended by the Lusignans. The lower ward housed the garrison and their horses. A tunnel leads on to the middle ward and a small Byzantine church. Some steps descend to a hall, which may have been a refectory, or banqueting chamber. Adjacent is a belvedere and café. The view over the coast is exceptional.

The path to the upper ward climbs steadily to the mountain top. Even then not everything is accessible, although St John's tower in its precipitous location can be reached by a short detour. The Queen's window is perhaps the place to stop and rest.

From a distance the battlements have a fairytale quality, inspiring thoughts of princesses and gallant knights

9
Salamis

In legend the founder of Salamis was the Greek hero Teucer, brother of Ajax, and son of Telamon. An impressive archaeological site.

In the 7th century BC Salamis was the first City of Cyprus. It was not until the Roman occupation centuries later that it was succeeded by Pafos in the west. In AD 350 the Byzantines changed the city's name to Constantia, and restored its status as the capital. There was much subsequent rebuilding due to earthquakes, but in the 7th century attacks by Arabs left the city in ruins.

In high summer a visit is a memorable occasion, although only the most determined will be able to stay the full course in the great heat. However, the Roman Theatre should not be missed, with its restored tiers of seats rising to an impressive height.

A little further north are the vents and hypocausts of the Baths, opening on to the Gymnasium, all built by the Romans. This structure, its rows of marble columns plainly evident, was damaged by earthquakes and remodelled in Byzantine times, only to collapse later. The columns that we see today were erected as recently as the 1950's.

 29E3

 10km north of Famagusta

8–8 (or sunset), main entrance closes 3:30, use north side entrance

Café near north entrance (£)

Cheap

Columns of the Gymnasium silhouetted against rare storm clouds

South of the Theatre the huge columns of the Granite Forum lie across the site. To the east are the few remains of the church of Agios Epifanios, built in the 4th century. This northern section of the site was a cultural centre. The Agora is found in the central part, near the Voutra, a 7th-century cistern. Close by are the unimpressive ruins of the Temple of Zeus.

It is a walk of some 500m northeast, towards the sea, to find the Kampanopetra, a large early Christian Basilica which has been only partially excavated. The Ancient Harbour is about 300m southeast, on the shoreline. Alternatively, cross the main road and walk about 200m to the western site. Here, at the Royal Necropolis, are several important tombs. These were designed for rich citizens, although there are also tombs for ordinary people near by, called the Cellarka.

10
Troodos

✝ 28C2

Central Cyprus

Cafés at Troodos village, Platres, Foini, Kakopetria and other villages (£–££)

Despite their elevation, these are friendly rounded hills with a multitude of charming villages hidden in the pine covered folds.

The Troodos is an extensive area, running from west of Larnaka to the high ground of Mount Olympus, then falling gradually to the western coast. There are many reasons for taking in the delights of the mountains, and they make a refreshing change from the hot beaches and dusty lowlands. Terraced vineyards shape the lower southern slopes, with Aleppo pine covering the higher ground.

Prodromos in springtime, the highest village in Cyprus

Summits may be tree covered or adorned with spiky scrub, relieved occasionally with dried flowers. Northern slopes are different again, dark poplars stand out in the valleys alongside golden oak and rock rose. Summer days are cooler on the high ground and a big attraction in winter is the snow, with skiing on Mount Olympus.

The most impressive of Cyprus's celebrated monasteries are in the Troodos. Chrysorrogiatissa (➤ 62), standing in splendid terrain, is about 45km from Pafos. Kykkos (➤ 20) is more convenient for Limassol, but still half a day's excursion. In the east is Machairas (➤ 80), less splendid, but well worth a visit.

Regrettably few seek out the small Byzantine churches of Panagia tou Araka (➤ 81) and Stavros tou Agiasmati near Lagoudera on the north side of the range. This is understandable, because it is a long drive, but the paintings are extraordinary.

These days walks and trails are popular in Cyprus, and those above Platres (Kaledonia Falls) are detailed in a colourful booklet produced by the tourist office.

In western Cyprus the forest takes over, and Cedar Valley (➤ 12) is renowned for its giant timbers. Fortunately for the peace of this marvellous area few people seem prepared to negotiate the difficult roads.

What To See

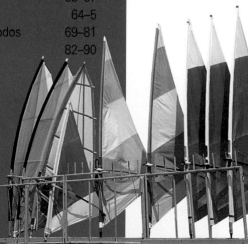

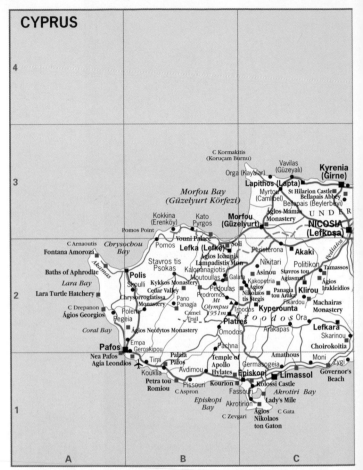

CYPRUS

4

3

C Kormakitis
(Koruçam Burnu)

Vavilas
(Güzelyalı)

**Kyrenia
(Girne)**

Orga (Kayalar)

Lapithos (Lapta)

Myrtou
(Çamlıbel)

St Hilarion Castle

Bellapais Abbey

*Morfou Bay
(Güzelyurt Körfezi)*

Bellapais (Beylerbeyi)

U N D E R

**Morfou
(Güzelyurt)**

Ágios Mamas
Monastery

**NICOSIA
(Lefkoşa)**

Kokkina
(Erenköy)

Kato
Pyrgos

Soli

Pomos Point

Lefka (Lefke)

Peristerona

Akaki

C Arnaoutis

*Chrysochou
Bay*

Pomos

Fontana Amoroza

Ágios Ioánnis
Lampadistis Mon.

Nikitari

Politikon

Tamassos

Stavros tis
Psokas

Kalopanagiotis

Asinou

Stavros tou
Agiasmáti

Akamas

Baths of Aphrodite

Moutoullas

Galata

**Ágios
Irakleidios**

Lara Bay

Polis

Kykkos Monastery

Pedoulas

Ágios
Nikolaos
tis Stegis

Panagia
tou Araka

Lara Turtle Hatchery

Stroulli

Cedar Valley

Prodromos

Fikardou

Klirou

**Machairas
Monastery**

Chrysorrogiatissa
Monastery

Pano
Panagia

*Mt
Olympus
1951m*

Kyperounta

Ora

C Drepanon

Camel
Trail

Troódos

T r o ó d o s

Lefkara

Ágios Georgios

Pegeia

Platres

Arakapas

Skarinou

Coral Bay

Ágios Neofytos Monastery

Omodos

Pachna

Choirokoitia

Pafos

Empa
Geroskipou

Palaia
Pafos

Amathous

Moni

Nea Pafos
Agía Leondios

Tími

Avdímou

Temple of
Apollo
Hylates

Germasogeia

Zygi

Kouklia

Episkopi

Limassol

**Governor's
Beach**

**Petra tou
Romiou**

Pissouri

C Aspron

Kourion

Kolossi Castle

Fassouri

Akrotiri Bay

*Episkopi
Bay*

Akrotirion

Lady's Mile

Ágios
Nikolaos
ton Gaton

C Gata

C Zevgari

A   **B**   **C**

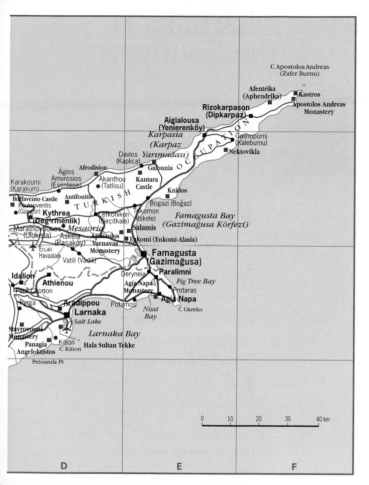

C Apostolos Andreas
(Zafer Burnu)

Afentrika
(Aphendrika)
Kastros

Rizokarpason
(Dipkarpaz)
Apostolos Andreas
Monastery

Aigialousa
(Yenierenköy)

Karpasia
(Karpaz)
Yarımadası)

O C C U P A T I O N

Galinoporni
(Kaleburnu)

Davlos
(Kaplıca)
Yarımadası
Nektovikla

Ágios
Amvrosios
(Esentepe)
Afrodision
Galounia

Karakoumi
(Karakum)
Akanthou
(Tatlısu)
Kantara
Castle

Buffavento Castle
Koutsoventis
(Güngör)
Antifonitis
Knidos

T U R K I S H

Kythrea
(Değirmenlik)
Lefkonikon
(Geçitkale)
Bogazi (Boğaz)

Trikomon
(İskele)

Famagusta Bay
(Gazimağusa Körfezi)

Marathovounos
(Ulukışla)
Mesaoria
Salamis

Askeia
(Paşaköy)
Apostolos
Varnavas
Enkomi (Enkomi-Alasia)

Ercan
Havaalanı
Vatili (Vadili)
Monastery
Famagusta
(Gazimağusa)

Idalion
Deryneia
Paralimni

Athienou
Agia Napa
Monastery
Fig Tree Bay

Pyrga Choirion

Potamos
Protaras

Pyrga
Agia Napa

Aradippou
Nissi
Bay
C Gkreko

Larnaka

Stavrovouni
Monastery
Salt Lake

Panagia
Angeloktistos
Kition
C Kition
Larnaka Bay

Hala Sultan Tekke

Petounda Pt

0   10   20   30   40 km

D   E   F

Looking west along the
rocky shore from Cape
Gkreko

29

Larnaka &
the Southeast

This part of Cyprus was once its agricultural heartland and it still provides the bulk of the Cypriot potato crop, which thrives in the distinctive red soil. However, in the last 20 years the agricultural industry has been supplanted by tourism, focused on two, previously quiet, resorts – Agía Napa and Protaras. The growth of these areas has been dramatic – in 1974 Agía Napa provided tourists with 126 beds, today that figure is 14,000.

Beaches are the main attraction of this region, and the coastline offers a good range of places worth stopping at, although the crowds tend to descend on summer weekends. The other attractions of the area are more low key; some traditional villages, Larnaka, the only settlement of any size, and a glimpse of the 'forbidden city' of Famagusta.

'If you blew your nose loudly in Larnaca before driving at speed to Limassol you would almost certainly meet someone on arrival who had already heard of the fact.'

LAWRENCE DURRELL
Bitter Lemons of Cyprus (1957)

Larnaka

Larnaka is a significant tourist and commercial centre and is a very convenient base for exploring the island, although its own sites of interest are fairly limited. The modern city is built on the remains of ancient Kition which was, according to the legend, established by one of Noah's grandsons in the 13th century BC. Out of this settlement Larnaka became an important trading centre, from where the island's main export of copper was shipped, and it has long had a large foreign population.

The town can be very busy at rush hour and the narrow streets and one way system do not help the foreign driver. Visitors should try to park quickly and explore on foot. The pedestrianised seafront is lined with cafés and at the far end of the promenade is a large marina with berths for 450 yachts. Larnaka is the main yachting centre of the island and the port facilities here attract boats from all over the eastern Mediterranean. There is a very popular beach in the centre of town, but it is man-made and it is certainly not among the best on the island. The seafront road provides amenities for the captive tourist market with an abundance of cafés, restaurants and ice-cream sellers.

Larnaka has a long history, but much of the evidence of that history has been covered by the sprawl of the modern city. However the enthusiastic will be able to track down archaeological remains and historic churches.

Larnaka's town beach is conveniently located by the main promenade

31

What to See in Larnaka

ÁGIOS LAZAROS CHURCH ✪✪

The legend states that Lazaros, having been raised from the dead by Christ, came to Larnaka to live out the rest of his days and when he definitively died he was buried here. His remains, however, were stolen and only his empty tomb is visible in the south apse. The church itself was built in the 9th century and was then extensively restored in the 17th century, including the decoration of its extremely ornate interior.

ARCHAEOLOGICAL MUSEUM ✪

This museum has a good range of exhibits from the local sites of Kition and Khirokitia, some of which date back as far as 3000 BC. The first room contains statues and terracotta figurines. The second room houses the pottery collection, along with some Mycenaean vases. Several other rooms contain neolithic artefacts, including the reconstruction of a neolithic tomb, and finally some Roman glassware. The museum's pleasant garden contains a large number of fragments of statues and a circular mosaic pavement.

Ágios Lazaros Church

✚ 32B1
✉ Agiou Lazarou Street
⏰ Daily, still used as a church
🍴 Cafés near by (££)
👆 Free

Archaeological Museum

✚ 32B2
✉ Kalograion Street
☎ 04 630169
⏰ Mon–Wed, Fri 7:30–2:30, Thurs 7:30–2:30, 3–6 (not in Jul–Aug). Closed 1 Jan, 25 Dec
🍴 Cafés near by (£)
👆 Cheap

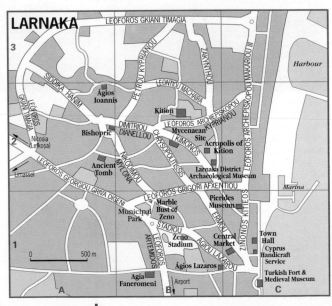

KITION ✪✪

The remains of the ancient city can be found at a number of sites. The most visible ruins are on Leontiou Machaira near the Archaeological Museum. The trenches and walls date from the 12th and 13th centuries BC, when they enclosed the city. It is also possible to make out the traces of a Phoenician temple, and the sharp eyed may be able to detect images of ships carved into the south wall.

✚ 32B2
✉ Leontiou Machaira Street
🕐 Mon–Wed, Fri 7:30–2:30, Thur 7:30–2:30, 3–6 (not Jul–Aug). Closed 1 Jan, 25 Dec
🖐 Cheap

The main site at Kition – much of its stone was shipped to Egypt to build the Suez Canal

PIERIDES MUSEUM ✪✪

This museum was founded in 1974 to house the private collection of antiquities of Demetrius Pierides, covering the neolithic to the medieval period. The collection, of 3,600 exhibits, is housed in the Pierides family's fine 19th-century house, and contains early pottery decorated with some interesting designs, artefacts from the site at Marion, mainly jugs and vases, and one of the most important collections of Roman glassware and jewellery in Europe. The main hall has some early maps of Cyprus and artefacts relating to Cypriot folklore.

✚ 32C1
✉ Zinonos Kitieos Street
☎ 04 651345
🕐 Mon–Fri 9–1, 3–6, Sat 9–1, Sun 10–1. Closed 1 Jan, 25 Dec, Greek Orthodox Sun
🍴 Cafés near by (£)
🖐 Moderate

TURKISH FORT AND MEDIEVAL MUSEUM ✪

The fort was built in 1625 by the Turks to defend the city against raiders but was soon adapted for use as a prison. It now serves as a small medieval museum, featuring mainly suits of armour. There are also some artefacts from Kition and other excavations in the area. In summer theatrical performances sometimes take place in the courtyard.

✚ 32C1
✉ Larnaka seafront, south end of Ankara Street
🕐 Mon, Tue, Wed, Fri 7:30–5, Thu 7:30–6. Closed 1 Jan, 25 Dec
🍴 Cafés near by (££)
🖐 Cheap

Did you know ?

Zeno, the founder of the Stoic philosophy was born here. However, he spent most of his life teaching in Athens, where he lived to the extraordinary age of 98. He died, not of old age, but by committing suicide, presumably unable to be stoical any longer.

A Walk Around Larnaka

Distance
2km

Time
1–2 hours

Start/end point
The Marina
✚ 32C2
🚌 18

Lunch
Old Mansion Archontiko (£)
✉ 24 Athinon Avenue
☎ 04 655905

The walk starts at the northern end of the seafront by the marina.

Head inland on Pavlou Street, passing the tourist office before turning left into Zinonos Kitieos Street.

This is the main shopping street of Larnaka. It also contains the Pierides Museum, which houses an enormous and very varied range of historical artefacts from all over Cyprus (▶ 33).

Pass the yellow building of the Armenian Church and later the municipal market at the corner of Ermou Street. There is a very confusing maze of intersections at the end of Zinonos Kitieos Street requiring a sharp right and then follow the road round to the left.

The old mosque which is passed is now a youth hostel in the Laiki Geitonia. A little further (about five minutes) is Ágios Lazaros Church (▶ 32).

After exploring the church and its graveyard, head back towards the seafront down Agiou Lazarou Street.

This was once the Turkish part of town and the minaret of Djami Kebir mosque can be seen. Although it is still used by visiting Muslims, it is open to the public when services are not taking place.

Follow the main road back to the shore, and Larnaka fort is to the right (▶ 33).

It is worth pausing for a moment to take in the view from the south of the fort, where the coastline stretches away in a long strip of tourist development.

The campanile of Ágios Lazaros Church

It is a straight walk along the seafront, or along the beach, back to the marina.

What to See in the Southeast

AGÍA NAPA MARINE LIFE MUSEUM ⭐

This museum was opened in 1992 to display the marine life of Cyprus. The exhibits include a large number of fossils from prehistoric periods up to 220 million years ago. There is also an extensive collection of shells found in local waters; sea urchins; starfish; and local corals. Exhibits relating to the sea turtles, for which Cyprus is famous, can also be found. Photographs and specimens of current day sea life conclude the exhibition.

✚	29E2
✉	25 Agias Mavris Street
☎	03 721179
🕐	May–Sep, Mon, Thu 9–2, 4–6:30, Tue, Wed, Fri, Sat 9–2; Oct–Apr, Mon, Thu 9–2, 3–5:30, Tue, Wed, Fri, Sat 9–2
🍴	Many cafés near by (££)
🎟	Cheap

AGÍA NAPA MONASTERY ⭐⭐

Agía Napa is a major tourist resort but the centre of the village retains some charm by virtue of its monastery and its well watered gardens which present a welcome haven from the bustle outside. Its church was built in the 16th century over a cave in which an icon of the Virgin Mary was supposedly found. In the 17th century the monastery became very rich, owning much of the land in the area. It fell into disrepair during the 18th century and was abandoned, but was later restored under British rule and now belongs to the World Council of Churches.

✚	29E2
✉	Centre of Agía Napa village
🕐	Daily
🍴	Many cafés nearby (££)
🎟	Free

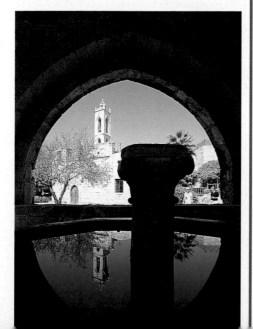

The still waters of the central fountain reflect the monastery, a sharp contrast to the frenetic activity outside

A Drive Around Cape Gkreko

Distance
135km

Time
3–5 hours

Start/end point
Larnaka Town Centre
 32B2

Lunch
Harbour-side fish restaurants
(££)
✉ Agía Napa

This drive runs east from Larnaka town centre, following the main road to the British base of Dhekalia.

Turn right into the base, passing through checkpoints at either end. At the other side of the base the road returns to the shoreline.

There are a number of good beaches along this road, as well as the village of Zylofagou. Close by is Potamos Creek (➤ 40), a delightful little fishing harbour with a safe – and usually quiet – beach.

The main road leads directly into Agía Napa, or there is an older, quieter route which runs closer to the shoreline – turn right off the main road, and then left to pass the beaches of Makronisos, Nissi and Sandy Bay (➤ 40).

Agía Napa harbour lies 1km east of Nissi. Another good sandy beach stretches away from the harbour out to the headland, where the cliffs have been carved by the water into spectacular formations. Agía Napa, the most popular destination in this area, lies just uphill. The many attractions here include a splendid marine life museum (➤ 35), a Luna Park, Skycoasters and Waterworld, an exciting water-based theme park (➤ 108). More sedate visitors can go instead to the ancient monastery in the village.

The route continues east on the Paralimni road. Once outside Agía Napa, turn off to follow the signs to Cape Gkreko.

There are good views from the cape and from the main road, which leads to Protaras (➤ 41). Beyond Protaras there are numerous small coves which offer pleasant, safe swimming.

Turn left through Paralimni and then complete the round trip by heading back towards Sotira, Liopetri and Zylofagou, where the road rejoins the main route to Larnaka.

The fine white sands of Nissi Beach are lapped by a clear, turquoise sea

Food & Drink

Cyprus has plenty of fresh produce and meat and the visitor should take the opportunity to make the most of the fruit which is so plentiful in the summer months. Quite apart from the well-known crops of the citrus fruits, there are peaches, plums, cherries, the ubiquitous melon and bananas – all easily available in season. Water melons, in particular, are sold from roadside stalls.

The wine suits most palates, zivania and ouzo are potent distillations so treat with caution

Greek Cuisine

The old staples of Greek cuisine, *moussaka*, *stifado*, kebab and Greek salad will be much in evidence. The *meze* is perhaps a good way to get an insight into Cypriot food. *Meze*, or *mezedhes*, is a series of small different dishes which are provided throughout an evening, and may cover absolutely everything or pursue a fish or a meat theme. In a good restaurant the *meze* can contain up to 30 different dishes, and it is important to pace yourself through the meal.

Kebab (*souvlaki*) appears on all menus, and lamb is another common dish on offer, either lamb chops or the more traditional *kleftiko*, which consists of large pieces of lamb baked slowly in traditional *kleftiko* ovens. Cypriots also have a taste for smoked meats, with the traditional *loukanika* sausage a favourite.

Fish is expensive, although *kalamari* – squid cooked in batter – is good value and widely available. Other fish options include swordfish, red mullet (*barbouni* in Greek), whitebait and sea bass. Alternatively, fresh trout is on the menu in some of the mountain villages.

Halloumi cheese is the main dairy product distinctive to the island. It is made from goat's milk and is often served

grilled. It is the food which the many expatriate Cypriots living in Britain claim they miss the most.

Visitors should seek out some of the cake shops which attract local custom. The traditional Greek desserts such as *baklava* and *cadefi* may be too sweet for some tastes but the wide range of custard-based cakes should appeal to all, as will the biscuits which can be bought by weight in these shops.

Interesting produce for sale outside Kykkos Monastery includes soujoukko for those with a sweet tooth.

A similar range of food is available in the Turkish part of the island. Some dishes such as *sis kebab*, *cacik* (cucumber and yoghurt salad), will already be familiar, but there are many other delights, among them *elma dizmesi*, a dish of apples and meat patties, and *cuvecte yaz turlusu*, a tasty summer stew.

Wine, Brandy and Beer

Cyprus wine is plentiful and cheap, and it is claimed that it has been made in Cyprus since 2000 BC. The main wineries are at Limassol, but increasingly smaller scale producers are growing up and some of the villages and monasteries now produce their own wines. It is an important export with 5 million gallons a year being exported to the United Kingdom alone.

Commandaria sweet wine is one of Cyprus's best known wines and it is claimed that it was drunk during the old festivals of Aphrodite. However, its origins can only be definitively traced back to the estate of the Knights Hospitaller at Kolossi, 700 years ago.

The island also produces brandy, and brandy sour is a popular tourist drink; it combines the local brandy with lemons and angostura bitters. Keo and Carlsberg beers are made locally and provide an alternative to the wines.

DERYNEIA ✪

This village gives an insight into recent Cypriot history. It is the nearest settlement to Famagusta and one villager has set up a viewing point where tourists, for a small fee, can climb up to the roof of his house and look through a telescope across no man's land to the closed city of Famagusta. Deryneia is also the place where trouble flared up in 1996 and two Greek Cypriots were killed whilst approaching the Turkish military zone.

HALA SULTAN TEKKE AND SALT LAKE (➤ 17, TOP TEN)

> *Did you know ?*
>
> Some 256sq km of Cyprus is
> British territory, contained within the three
> main military bases at Dhekalia, Akrotiri
> and Episkopi. These areas are
> subject to British law and are officially known
> as Sovereign Base Areas.

NISSI BEACH ✪✪✪

Nissi Beach is where tourist development in this area started. It is a pleasant sandy beach, although it can be very crowded in summer, with a rocky island just offshore. The existence of a sand bar makes it possible to wade to the island, an adventure which appeals especially to children. Those going to the island should, however, bear in mind that it is made up of some very spiky rocks and suitable footwear is necessary.

PANAGIA ANGELOKTISTOS CHURCH ✪✪
(KITION CHURCH)

Panagia Angeloktistos, which means 'built by angels', was constructed in the 11th century on the remains of an earlier 5th-century church. It has many ornate icons but its main attraction is its mosaic, which depicts angels attending the Virgin Mary as she holds Christ. It is a very intricate design and of a style not found anywhere else in Cyprus. The mosaic will be lit up for visitors on request.

POTAMOS ✪✪

This is a pleasant creek which serves as a small fishing harbour. At the shoreline there is a café and a long, if slightly rocky, beach with the church of Ágios Georgios at

---

Sidebar (left column):

✚ 29E2
✉ 11km north of Agía Napa
🍴 Café in village (£), restaurant on road to Paralimni (££)
🚌 From Protaras, in summer every hour 8–3, Sun last bus 1:30

✚ 29E2
✉ 2km west of Agía Napa
🍴 Several cafés (£)

✚ 29D2
✉ Edge of the village on road to Mazotos
🕐 Mon–Sat 8–4, Sun 9–12, 2–4. If locked ask for the key at the nearby café
🍴 Café near by (£)
🚌 From Larnaka
 Donation requested

✚ 29E2
✉ 14km west of Agía Napa
🍴 Café on beach (£)

its western end. Early in the morning, when the fishermen are returning with their catch, it is a lovely place. The beach is usually quiet and offers the opportunity for calm, safe swimming.

PROTARAS ✪✪

Protaras, also known as Fig Tree Bay because of the fig tree which was once its only landmark, is a fully fledged resort full of hotels, restaurants and the ubiquitous discos. The beach is sandy and there are very good watersports facilities. The offshore rocky islet offers the chance of some small degree of seclusion although you have to be a fairly strong swimmer to reach it

🚩 29E2
✉ 8km north of Cape Gkreko on east coast
🍴 Numerous cafés and restaurants (£–££)
🚌 From Agía Napa in summer: every hour 9–5, Sun 10–5

STAVROVOUNI ✪✪

The monastery of Stavrovouni is set at a height of 690m and the views from the top of the hill are spectacular. There has been a religious community here since AD 327 when St Helena brought a fragment of the Cross from Jerusalem. It is claimed that the piece is still in the monastery, covered by a silver casing. The original buildings were destroyed by Arab and Turkish raiders and those visible today date mainly from the 17th century. They are still occupied by a devout community of monks and women are not allowed inside.

🚩 29D2
✉ 40 km west of Larnaka
🕐 Daily to men only, Apr–Aug 8–12, 3–6; Sep–Mar 8–12, 2–5
🎟 Free

The chapel at Stavrovouni, with the barren landscape of Larnaka district in the distance

Limassol &
the South

This region has something for all tastes and all interests: an attractive coastline; a medieval castle; spectacular views; archaeological remains and, for the mythologically inclined, the birthplace of Aphrodite. Those with an interest in history will find plenty to occupy them. The 9,000 year-old site at Khirokitia is the oldest settlement on the island whilst Kourion and its restored amphitheatre has relics from the Mycenaean, Persian and Roman periods. There are links with ancient mythology too, a temple to Apollo and Petra tou Romiou, the place where Aphrodite is supposed to have emerged from the foaming sea. A newer tradition, only 500 years old, can be found in the lacemaking village of Lefkara and beyond Limassol are the vital ingredients for any Cypriot holiday, some good beaches.

> ❦

> *' They say Limassol is as large again as it was before the occupation and certainly it gives one the impression of being almost a new town. Houses are springing up everywhere, almost by magic. '*

ANONYMOUS
BRITISH ARMY OFFICER
stationed in Cyprus in 1882

Limassol

Limassol's main claim to fame is that Richard the Lionheart was shipwrecked here and married his fiancée Berengaria in the town. The Knights Templar then developed Limassol as a trading post based on export of the Commandaria wine which they made in the vineyards surrounding Kolossi. However, it was only in the 19th century that its major asset, the deep water port, began to be appreciated and the town grew into a significant commercial centre.

In recent years Limassol has seen massive tourist development and there is a line of hotels along each approach road. It is a modern town – new building and road works proliferate – but it does not lack atmosphere and offers good shopping, nightlife and restaurants. The carnival in spring and the wine festival in early September are particularly lively times to visit the town.

The sites of Limassol are easily explored on foot, indeed those coming by car should be prepared for traffic problems and a fiendishly complicated one-way system. The main historical site is the castle and medieval museum. There are also a couple of mosques, with distinctive minarets, serving as reminders of a time when Limassol had a Turkish sector. The main shopping area is around Agiou Andreou Street.

Agiou Andreou Street, once bustling with traffic, now a pedestrianised shopping haven

What to See in Limassol

AMATHOUS ✪✪

28C1

8km east of Limassol

Mon–Sat 7:30–5, Sun 10–4

From Limassol and Larnaka

Cheap

Ancient pavements and pillars of the Agora

The archaeological remains of Amathous are spread over a wide area and include a rock-cut tomb in the grounds of the Amathus Beach Hotel.

The most easily accessible ruins are of the Agora in a fenced site, just off the main road on the inland side. This was the market area and although it is a relatively small site there are a large number of pillars still visible which make it quite an impressive place. Up a track from the Agora is the Acropolis and the remains of a Temple to Aphrodite. There is evidence that some of the site is now underwater which offers exciting opportunities for snorkellers to explore.

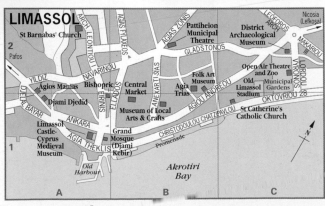

CASTLE AND MEDIEVAL MUSEUM ✪✪

The main buildings of the castle were constructed in the 14th century on the site of an earlier Byzantine structure. The chapel in which Richard the Lionheart and Berengaria were married was part of the original castle but is no longer standing. It was then used by the Turks as a prison and later by the British as the army headquarters.

The Cyprus Medieval Museum is now housed here. The basement contains replicas of sculptures and photographs of the Byzantine churches of Cyprus. Upstairs the exhibits are found in small rooms off a central hall with the most interesting items, the suits of armour and weapons, on the second floor. The final flight of stairs leads out on to the battlements where there are good views of the city. The most distinctive sights on the skyline are the two mosques, Djami Djedid and Djami Kebir, reminders that this was once the Turkish part of town.

✝ 44A1
✉ Eirinis Street, near the old port
☎ 05 330419
🕐 Mon–Fri 7:30–5, Sat 9–5. Closed 1 Jan, 25 Dec
🍴 Many cafés near by (£)
✋ Cheap

DISTRICT ARCHAEOLOGICAL MUSEUM ✪

The garden contains a sundial which supposedly belonged to Lord Kitchener. Inside, Room 1 contains neolithic tools and pottery from Amathous and Kourion. These artefacts are very old with some dating back to 2300 BC. Room 2 has later figurines and Roman coins. The final room contains some important statues from Amathous including those of Artemis and the Egyptian god, Bes.

✝ 44C2
✉ Kanningos and Vyronos Street
☎ 05 330132
🕐 Mon–Fri 7:30–5, Sat 9–5, Sun 10–1. Closed 1 Jan, 25 Dec, Greek Orthodox Easter Sun
🍴 Cafés (£) ✋ Cheap

MUNICIPAL GARDENS AND ZOO ✪✪

The Municipal Gardens offer some welcome greenery in a dusty city. It also contains a small zoo, although the animals are kept in very poor conditions. There is a small open-air theatre where there are productions during the summer. The Gardens are also the site of the annual Limassol Wine Festival, held in September. All the local wine companies set up stalls and offer an evening of wine tasting accompanied by music and dancing.

✝ 44C2
✉ 28 Oktovriou Street
🕐 Gardens: daylight hours; Zoo: daily 9–1, 2:30–6:30
🍴 Café in the gardens (£)
✋ Gardens: free; Zoo: moderate

The Gardens are a cool oasis

Limassol Walk

Distance:
2.5 km

Time:
1–3½ hours

Start point
Sea front car park
➕ 44B1

End point
Municipal gardens
➕ 44C1

Lunch
There are many cafés
opposite the castle (£)
✉ Eirinis Street

This walk starts on the seafront by the car park. The promenade is followed southwest to reach a small round-about which marks the old harbour, complete with its fishing boats. There is a small reptile house on one corner with a collection of local and foreign species.

Proceed inland to the 14th-century Castle and Medieval Museum (➤ 45). Turn right along Genthliou Mitella Street and pass a mosque which is still in use.

This was once the Turkish part of the town and many of the older houses are of a typical Turkish design. The municipal fruit and vegetable market lies just east of the mosque.

Continue generally northeast until the road leads into Agiou Andreou Street, the main shopping street (➤ 106).

Did you know ?

It is claimed that wine has been made in Cyprus for 4,000 years. There are four wineries in Limassol run by Keo, Etko, Loel and Sodap. The wine with longest history is the Commandaria which Richard the Lionheart called 'the wine of kings and the king of wines'.

There are many narrow alleyways in this area, but they are interesting to explore and walkers should not worry about getting lost as they will eventually emerge on to the wider thoroughfare. Agiou Andreou has a wide range of shops ranging from the usual souvenirs to leather goods and jewellery.

After about 1km Agía Trias Church can be visited a short way up Agias Triados Street, just before Zinonos Street. Returning to the main road the Folk Art Museum is found a little way on, and to the left. One kilometre further along Agiou Andreou Street, at the north side of the municipal gardens, turn right on Kanningkos Street to reach the Archaeological Museum (➤ 45), 200m to the left. The walk ends in the municipal gardens, which offer relief from the busy city streets.

What to See in the South

AKROTIRI PENINSULA   ✪✪

The area contains a good beach, a salt lake and a historic church. In summer the salt lake, has a distinctive grey colour and the visitor can smell the salt; in winter it fills with water and is a stopping off point for passing flamingoes. Lady's Mile beach is sandy and offers safe swimming in very shallow sea. The far end is closed off, marking the start of the British Base at Akrotiri and the occasional military jet may disturb the peace.

The church of Ágios ton Gaton (St Nicholas of the Cats) is reached on a track at the southern end of the beach. It was founded in AD 325, although the buildings seen today were constructed in the 13th century and have been restored since. The cats in its name are still much in evidence.

AVDIMOU BEACH   ✪✪

Avdimou beach is a really good long sandy stretch although the water becomes deep very quickly. There is a small café at its eastern end and it is usually quiet, although at weekends it can be busy with servicemen and their families. It is part of the British Sovereign Base and so has not seen any tourist development.

GOVERNOR'S BEACH   ✪✪

The beach is reached down some steps cut out of the tall white cliffs. The astonishingly dark sand is its most distinctive feature and can get painfully hot by the middle of a summer's day. The beach, although narrow, is popular with local people and can be very busy on summer weekends.

✚ 28C1
🐾 Ágios Nikolaos ton Gaton (St Nicholas of the Cats): daily. Closed during siesta
🍴 Cafés on beach (£)
🎟 Free

✚ 28B1
✉ 3km off main road, opposite turning to Avdimou village
🍴 Café on beach (£)

✚ 28C1
✉ Junction 16 Nicosia to Limassol motorway
🍴 Cafés on clifftop (£)

Governor's Beach, dark sands and white cliffs

➕ 20C2

✉ Off Junction 14,
Nicosia–Limassol
motorway

🕐 Mon–Fri 7:30–5, Sat–Sun
9–5. Closed 1 Jan,
25 Dec, Greek Orthodox
Easter Sun

✋ Cheap

KHIROKITIA ✪

This is the oldest archaeological site on the island, dating from 6800 BC when it was home to 2,000 people who farmed the surrounding land.

The most distinctive feature of the settlement is the beehive shaped houses which came in two sizes, one about 4m across and the other 8m. They were built close together and linked by narrow passageways, and it was obviously a very crowded settlement. The inhabitants tended to bury their dead under the floor of the house and then build on top and some houses have revealed up to eight different periods of habitation.

The settlement is best explored by following the vestiges of the main street, with House A near the entrance being the easiest to make out. A second group of ruins has the remains of pillars visible which once supported the roof. From there the site becomes more complicated and the best views are from the top of the hill from where the wider perspective can reveal its layout.

➕ 28C1

✉ 14.5km from Limassol
town centre

🕐 Jun–Sep, daily 7:30–7:30;
Oct–May, daily 7:30–5.
Closed 1 Jan, 25 Dec,
Greek Orthodox Easter
Sun

🍴 Café on site (£)

🚌 From Limassol

✋ Cheap

KOLOSSI CASTLE ✪✪✪

Kolossi was the headquarters of the Knights Hospitaller, who probably built the first fort in the late 13th century. They exploited the fertile land in the area, using locally produced sugar and grapes to make Commandaria wine.

The castle suffered from a number of attacks by Mameluke raiders in the 14th century, and the buildings visible today date from rebuilding which took place in the 15th century. The Turks took it over in 1570 and sugar production continued until 1799.

Visitors pass over a drawbridge into a pleasant garden and then into the keep, which has walls 2.75m thick and is three storeys (23m) high. The defenders used to throw boiling oil from the machicoulis on to the attackers below.

Much of the ground floor was used as a storage area. The first floor has two large rooms and a kitchen. On the second floor were the apartments of the Grand Commander, which have a spacious, airy feel to them from four large windows. A spiral staircase leads on to the roof, from where there are good views. The large vaulted building in the grounds was the place where the sugar was made.

KOURION (► 18–19, TOP TEN)

LEFKARA ✪✪

The village is divided into two halves, Pano (upper) and Kato (lower) Lefkara and is a very popular tourist destination. Visitors who prefer to avoid the crowds come in the early morning.

Lefkara is known for its lace, called *lefkaritika*; and first became famous in 1481 when Leonardo da Vinci ordered some for Milan Cathedral. It then became popular with local Venetian ladies and the lacemaking industry took off. The tradition continues to flourish today and rather ferocious ladies will offer their wares vigorously to passing tourists. Those wishing to buy should take care to ensure that it is the genuine article and not imported. There are also a number of silverware shops.

The main street of Pano Lefkara is now designed to cater for tourists but the narrow alloys to either side are still peaceful places to wander. There is also a small museum of lacemaking and silverware, signposted uphill from the main street.

✚ 28C2
✉ 9km northwest of junction 13 of the Nicosia –Limassol motorway
☎ Museum: 04 342326
🕐 Museum: Mon–Sat 10–4
🍴 Cafés in the main street of the upper village (£)

The lower half of the village is often neglected but is worth a visit. Its church of Archangel Michael has some beautiful 18th-century icons and there are very good views across the hills from outside the building. The houses in this part of the village are painted in a distinctive blue and white and its streets extremely narrow and therefore traffic free.

A local lady patiently awaits the first trade of the day

49

➕ 28B1
✉ 24km east of Pafos
🍴 Two cafés, one in tourist pavilion (£)

PETRA TOU ROMIOU ✪✪✪

This is one of the most photographed sites on the whole island. The name means the Rock of Romios and the two large rocks in the sea, set against the white cliffs, provide a spectacular scene. There are two official places to stop – one close to the rock, just back from the shore, where there is a café and a car park, the other higher up in the cliffs, where there is a tourist pavilion. However, the best view, coming from Limassol, is on the final bend before the road starts to descend; some scrubland on the left makes a convenient layby.

Legend states that this was the birthplace of Aphrodite, where she emerged from the foaming water. The beach itself is rather shingly, and it is not ideal for swimming because it gets rough around the rocks, but it is worth stopping to soak up the mysterious atmosphere.

➕ 28B1
✉ Limassol–Pafos Road
🕐 Jun–Sep, daily 7:30–7:30; Oct–May, daily 7:30–5. Closed 1 Jan, 25 Dec, Greek Orthodox Easter Sun
✋ Cheap

TEMPLE OF APOLLO HYLATES ✪✪

The temple was first used as a place of pilgrimage in the 8th century BC although the ruins seen today are from AD 100, when it was rebuilt after an earthquake. There is a marked pathway and map to guide the visitor around the site. The circular remains of the votive pit are worth a closer look. These pits were used to store unwanted ritual gifts and archaeologists have found them a very rich source of artefacts. The pathway then leads to the Temple of Apollo, it has been partially restored and the high columns are a very striking reminder of ancient times.

The covered shed structure contains the Priest's House, and though you have to peer through the fence you can see some mosaics and pillars. The remaining buildings of interest are the Palaestra, which was an open space used for sporting activities, and a near by complex of Baths.

Drive from Limassol to Petra tou Romiou

The drive begins in Limassol town centre.

Head towards the new port, then turn west to Asomatos and Fassouri, passing through citrus groves.

The dense citrus groves around the village provide a pleasant drive, and guided tours are also available.

Turn north to Kolossi, a Lusignan Castle (➤ 48). After Kolossi village, turn left and in 2km the road passes through the village of Episkopi.

This village was founded in the 7th century by refugees from Kourion. More recently it has become home to British services personnel and their families from the nearby British base. From the village it is a short detour to the site of Kourion (➤ 18), the most impressive archaeological site in the south of the island.

Rejoin the main road, taking extreme care on the dangerous bends, and continue towards Pafos.

In about 1km, on the inland side of the road, is Kourion Stadium and after a further 2km is the Temple of Apollo Hylates, another very impressive place (➤ 50). Immediately beyond this, the road enters the British base of Episkopi, which lies at the bottom of a valley. Its green playing fields make a striking contrast with its dusty surroundings.

To the west of the base is a turning to 'Avdimou Beach' (➤ 47), opposite the turning to Avdimou village, lying 3km away on a very narrow track. The main route continues along the coast.

Pissouri, a few kilometres further, provides an alternative beach and the possibility of lunch in the village. Beyond here the road runs high in the cliffs, with some really spectacular scenery, but on a slow road.

Continue for another 6km to reach Petra tou Romiou, the legendary birthplace of Aphrodite.

Distance
65km

Time
1½–5 hours

Start point
Limassol town centre
 44B1

End point
Petra tou Romiou
28B1

Lunch
Bunch of Grapes (££)
 Pissouri Village
☎ 05 221275

Pafos & the West

This is the region for those looking for some of Cyprus's quieter and more traditional areas. Pafos is a growing resort but it has not lost its small town origins, or its hugely important archaeological heritage. In the north are monasteries and villages where the donkey is still a common mode of transport. Polis, the only town of any size on the north coast, is a laid back place. In the far northwest is the Akamas peninsula, which is the focus of environmental initiatives to protect some of the most remote and beautiful beaches in Cyprus. East of Polis is an undeveloped region with empty beaches and quiet roads up to the Green Line which marks the limit of exploration for visitors in the Greek sector of the island.

'Here [Pafos] the votaries of Aphrodite were welcomed from overseas. Here St Paul took ship after the happy outcome of his encounter with my prudent Roman predecessor. Here the crusaders and pilgrims came on their way to the Holy Land.'

SIR HUGH FOOT,
then Governor of Cyprus (1959)

Pafos

The first settlement here dates from the 4th century BC and Pafos played an important role in early Cypriot history. However, after the 4th century AD it declined and, although its fortunes improved under British administration, it is only in the last 30 years, as transport links improved, that Pafos has seen real growth. Tourist development, in particular, took off after the construction of the new international airport in 1983. However, the town remains of manageable size, with a resident population of 31,000, and is one of the most attractive holiday resorts on the island. The richness of its archaeological heritage has placed Pafos on UNESCO's list of World Cultural Heritage Sites.

The modern town is split into two; upper and lower Pafos, also known as Kitma and Kato Pafos. The lower part of town, on the coast, contains most of the historic sites whereas the upper town contains the main commercial centre, shops and modern museums. It needs to be borne in mind that it is quite a strenuous walk between the two parts of town, especially in the summer heat.

The lower town contains most of the archaeological remains which are spread out across the area. Some are in

Pafos harbour, a colourful spot for sitting or strolling

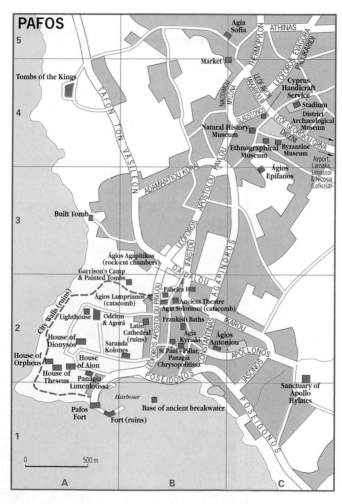

PAFOS

Agía Sofia
ATHINAS
THERMOPYLON
LEOFOROS EVAGORA PALLIKARIDI

Market

Tombs of the Kings

Cyprus Handicraft Service

Stadium

District Archaeological Museum

Natural History Museum

Ethnographical Museum

Byzantine Museum

Ágios Epifanos

Airport, Larnaka, Limassol & Nicosia (Lefkosa)

Built Tomb

Ágios Agapitikos (rock-cut chambers)

Garrison's Camp & Painted Tombs

Ágios Lamprianos (catacomb)

Lighthouse

Odelon & Agorá

Fabrica Hill

Ancient Theatre

Agia Solomoni (catacomb)

Frankish Baths

Latin Cathedral (ruins)

House of Dionysos

Saranda Kolones

Agia Kyriaki

Ágios Antoniou

House of Orpheus

House of Aion

House of Theseus

Panagia Limeloússá

St Paul's Pillar, Panagia Chrysopolitissa

Sanctuary of Apollo Hylates

Harbour

Base of ancient breakwater

Pafos Fort

Fort (ruins)

0   500 m

formal sites, but do not be surprised to come across ancient ruins amongst modern houses. The harbour is the focus of the lower town and is a pleasant place to stroll. It is also the haunt of Pafos's most famous resident; the pelican. Cafés are strung out along the sea front and there are plenty of places to stop and eat or have a drink and watch the yachts which still use the port.

What to See in Pafos

CATACOMBS

55B2
Apostolou Pavlou Avenue
Daylight hours
Free

There are two underground churches in Pafos. Agía Solomoni is easily identified from the road because those who believe in the magical curative powers of the tomb attach items of clothing to the tree outside. The underground chambers include a 12th-century chapel with frescoes, some of which were damaged by water and early graffiti left by passing Crusaders. The chambers are fairly dark and a torch might be useful, although the main chapel is lit by candles.

The second catacomb, a few minutes walk further north, is larger, but has been less well cared for and tends to be rather litter strewn.

Agía Solomoni and its famous tree bedecked with clothing

Facing page: Pafos lighthouse towers over the semicircle of restored limestone seats of the Roman Odeion

DISTRICT ARCHAEOLOGICAL MUSEUM

This museum houses most of the finds from local excavations. In the entrance hall is a Hellenistic sarcophagus from Pegeia and there is pottery and terracotta figures from Polis, a skeleton found at Lemba, small statues and artefacts from the House of Dionysos, sculpture and coins from the ancient city kingdoms of Cyprus. Most fascinating are articles found in room 3, ranging from marble Roman eyeballs to clay hot water bottles in the shape of the part of the body they were to warm.

➕ 55C4
✉ Dighenis Street
☎ 06 240215
🕐 Mon–Fri 7:30–2:30, 3–5 (till 6 Thu), Sat–Sun 10–1. Closed 1 Jan, 25 Dec, Greek Orthodox Easter Sun
🍴 Cafés across the road (£)
✋ Cheap

ETHNOGRAPHICAL MUSEUM

This is the private collection of George Eliades, a local professor, and covers the whole range of history from neolithic to modern times. The collection includes axe heads, coins, pottery and farm implements from around the island. There is also a reconstruction of a bridal chamber displaying traditional costumes and furniture.

➕ 55C4
✉ 1 Exo Vrisis Street
☎ 06 232010
🕐 May–Sep, Mon–Fri 9–1, 3–7, Sat 9–1, Sun 10–1; Oct–May, Mon–Fri 9–1, 2–5, Sat 9–1, Sun 10–1
🍴 Cafés near by (£)
✋ Cheap

MOSAICS (► 22, TOP TEN)

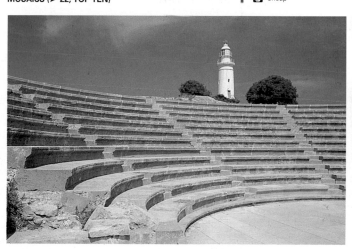

ODEION

This theatre has been partially restored to give an interesting impression of how it would have been. It was built in the 2nd century AD, during the Roman period, then suffered earthquake damage in the 7th century and was abandoned. Some performances are still put on here during the summer, and details are available from the tourist office.

Just in front of the Odeion is the Agora, once the city's market place. The foundations and some of the columns are still visible, and there are also remains of some other municipal buildings.

➕ 55A2
✉ West of Apostolou Pavlou Avenue
🕐 Daylight hours
🍴 Cafés near by on Apostolou Pavlou Avenue (£)
✋ Free

57

A Walk Around Pafos

Distance
3.5km

Time
1–4 hours

Start/end point
Pafos harbour
✠ 55A1
🚌 15 to Coral Bay

Lunch
There are a number of cafés
along the harbour (££)

*Pafos lighthouse is a
useful landmark when
exploring the
archaeological sites of
the Nea Pafos headland*

The walk begins at the fort at the far end of the harbour.
The fort was built by the Lusignans and the dungeons and
battlement are worth a visit (➤ 59).

*Head inland on to the scrubland towards the
modern lighthouse until reaching the tarred
road, then follow the signs to the mosaics.*

The mosaics are some of the most impressive in the world
and are amazingly well preserved (➤ 22). A little way back
down the hill, to the left, is the Odeion (➤ 57), the
restored Roman theatre dating from the 2nd century AD,
just to the east of the lighthouse.

*From the Odeion, take the track east towards
town, meeting the tarred road after five minutes
and soon after the main road of Apostolou
Pavlou Avenue. Turn left, and 200m away on
the right-hand side is the catacomb of Agia
Solomoni.*

The church is marked by a tree
covered in handkerchiefs and is in
the furthest cave.

*Return down Apostolou Pavlou
Avenue for about 4oom, turn
left into Stilis Agiou Pavlou
Street to reach the site of St
Paul's Pillar after about 200m.*

The pillar, visible through a fence,
is the site where St Paul was
whipped on the order of the Romans
(➤ 60).

*Return to Apostolou Pavlou
Avenue to go left. After 200m,
turn right on to the road signed
'Ancient Monuments'. On the
right is Saranda Kolones, a
ruined Byzantine fort (➤ 60).
Cross the car park to return to
the harbour.*

PAFOS FORTS ⊗⊗

Originally the harbour was guarded by two castles built by the Lusignans in the 13th century. Both were badly damaged when the Turks attacked in 1570, but one was subsequently restored and used by the Turks as a prison. It is now open to the public with access across a drawbridge. The main attractions are the dungeons and the battlements from where there are excellent views across the harbour.

🕂 55A1
✉ Harbour Wall
🕐 Mon–Wed, Fri 7:30–2:30, also Thu 7:30–2:30, 3–6, Sat–Sun 9–5. Closed 1 Jan, 25 Dec, Greek Orthodox Easter Sun
🍴 Cafés on harbour front (££)
👍 Cheap

The harbour's solid redoubt compliments any view over the still waters

Did you know ?

The ancient city of Pafos was destroyed twice by earthquakes. It has remained susceptible to tremors and in October 1996 a tremor measuring 6.1 on the Richter Scale was felt, causing landslides and some structural damage.

ST PAUL'S PILLAR AND AGÍA KYRIAKI ✪

🕇 55B2
✉ Stassandrou Street
🕐 Daylight hours
🍴 Cafés near by (£)
✋ Free

This is a small archaeological site in the back streets of Pafos where a large number of columns and other fragments of buildings have been unearthed. Excavations are still taking place and this may mean that parts of the site will be closed off. The archaeologists are not sure what the actual buildings were in this area, although one theory is that it was a Roman Forum. Most people, however, come here to see St Paul's Pillar which stands at the western end of the site. According to legend, St Paul was tied to this stone and given 39 lashes as a punishment for preaching Christianity. Despite this early setback, he later managed to convert the Governor and the rest of the island soon followed suit.

The adjacent church of Agía Kyriaki dates from the 12th century and is still used for services.

Intricately carved, and somewhat worse for wear, floral capital in the Byzantine Museum

Did you know ?

St Barnabas brought Christianity to Cyprus. Accompanied by St Paul, he landed at Salamis then travelled to Pafos. The story of their travels is told in Acts in the Bible, which relates how St Paul blinded a local sorcerer and so impressed the Roman consul of Pafos that he converted to Christianity

SARANDA KOLONES (FORTY COLUMNS) BYZANTINE FORT ✪✪

🕇 55B2
✉ Kyriakou Nikolaou Street
🕐 Open access
🍴 Cafés near by (££)
✋ Free

This castle dates from around the 7th century, although it was rebuilt in the 12th century, and was probably meant to protect the city from seaborne raiders until it was replaced by the forts on the breakwater. The remains of many of the original columns, the central keep and some of the towers on the thick outer walls can still be made out. Visitors can also see a drinking trough for horses and the ancient lavatories. The site is open to the public who are allowed to scramble freely around the ruins but those with young children should take care as some of the high walls could be dangerous.

TOMBS OF THE KINGS ✪✪

The 100 tombs on the site cover a wide area and are cut out of the ground with a steep drop into them, so visitors should take care when exploring. Steps lead down inside the tombs, often into a whole series of passageways. The chambers near the centre of the site do get busy and it is worth walking a little further away to those on the edge of the area, which are just as impressive. They are constructed with Doric columns, date from about the 3rd century BC and were probably used to bury the local noblemen and their families.

There are some good views over the sea and a few rocky coves are accessible after a bit of a scramble over the cliffs.

🟊 55A4
✉ 2km northwest of Pafos centre
☎ 06 240295
🕐 Mon–Fri 7:30–5, Sat–Sun 9–5
🍴 Café on site (£)
🚌 Regular bus service from Pafos
✋ Cheap

Exploring the tombs is something of an adventure

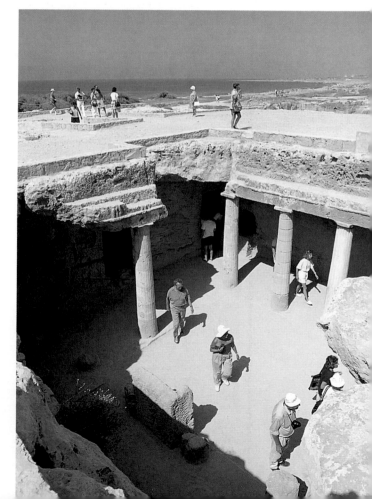

What to See in the West

ÁGIOS GEORGIOS

Ágios Georgios is a pleasant, quiet harbour with a couple of restaurants and rooms to rent. The whole area was once a Roman settlement and some of the tombs cut out of the rock can be seen. On the headland are the remains of a 6th-century basilica.

The harbour is reached down a track from the headland and signposted Mandoulis beach. It is a very pretty place with a good stretch of sand and a view to the rocky offshore island of Geronisos.

28A2
25km north of Pafos
Restaurants overlooking the harbour (£)

ÁGIOS NEOFYTOS MONASTERY

Saint Neofytos first set up residence in caves he cut out of the hillside in 1159. The first cave he created was called the *enkleistra*, or enclosure. He then enlarged the dwelling with the addition of three new chambers, which are decorated with religious wall paintings focusing on the Crucifixion and Resurrection. Those in the sanctuary, the cave with an altar, are the best preserved. The 16th-century monastery church is dedicated to the Virgin Mary and contains a large number of paintings which depict her early life. Neofytos's bones are also kept here in a wooden sarcophagus, with his skull in a silver receptacle which the devoted queue up to kiss.

28B2
9km north of Pafos
Daylight hours, access to the church limited during services
Two buses a day from Pafos old town
Free

AKAMAS (► 16, TOP TEN)

CHRYSORROGIATISSA MONASTERY

The monastery is impressive mainly because of its setting at a height of 610m. It was founded in 1152 by a monk called Ignatius, although the main part of the monastery

28B2
3km south of Pano Panagia
Daily 9–12:30, 3–sunset
Café outside monastery (£)
Free

A moment for contemplation in the impressive interior

was not built until 1770. These buildings were burnt down in 1821 when the Turks suspected the monks of political activity. Further trouble came in the 1950s when the Abbot was murdered by EOKA terrorists who thought, erroneously, he had betrayed some of their comrades.

The monks here have shown some enterprise in reopening an old winery and now produce some excellent wines, which are on sale in the monastery. They also have icons for sale, which are painted by one of the monks. Outside the main buildings is a small café.

CORAL BAY ✪

This is an increasingly popular resort, with shops and restaurants on the approach road and watersports facilities on the beach. The sands are clean and pleasant and can be painfully hot to bare feet. It can also be busy.

GEROSKIPOU ✪

The church of Agía Paraskevi, in the centre of the village, is famous throughout the island because of its distinctive five-domed style. Its main building dates from the 10th-century but it has a number of decorations over the altar from the 9th century. The paintings are slightly later, from the 12th to 15th century.

There is also a good Folk Art Museum just off the main street which contains farming and domestic implements and traditional costumes. The village is known for its Cyprus delight, Loukoumi (called Turkish delight before the Turkish invasion); and it is possible to watch it being made in some of the shops.

LARA (► 21, TOP TEN)

PALAIA PAFOS (OLD PAFOS) KOUKLIA ✪

The site, also known as the Sanctuary of Aphrodite, is spread over a large area. At the entrance is a restored Lusignan manor (La Cavocle) with substantial and impressive Turkish additions. It houses, in its main hall, a museum with exhibits focusing on the history of the excavation of the area and the fragments of mosaic which were found. Its prize artefact, though, is a large black stone which stood as a manifestation of Aphrodite and was worshipped by pilgrims. The hall itself is worth a closer look as it is one of the best examples of 13th-century Gothic architecture on the island.

To the east of the museum, Roman remains can be seen, including the remnants of the Sanctuary of Aphrodite which stands around a courtyard where the rituals took place. The south wing is the best preserved, and parts of the original walls can still be seen.

West of the sanctuary are the remains of Roman houses, including the House of Leda; follow the pathway which leads to a replica of a mosaic of Leda and the Swan.

✛ 28A2
⊠ 13km north of Pafos
🚌 Regular buses from Pafos old town
🍴 Cafés on the clifftops (££)

✛ 28B2
⊠ 3km east of Pafos
☎ 06 240216
◉ Folk Art Museum: Mon–Wed, Fri 7:30–2:30, Thu 7:30–2:30, 3–6 (not Jul–Aug)
🍴 Many cafés in village (£–££)
🚌 Regular buses from Pafos old town
♿ Folk Museum: cheap, church: free

✛ 28B1
⊠ 14km east of Pafos
☎ 06 432180
◉ Mon–Fri 7:30–5, Sat–Sun 9–4. Closed 1 Jan, 25 Dec, Greek Orthodox Easter Sun
♿ Museum: cheap; rest of the site: free

In the Know

If you only have a short time to visit Cyprus, or would like to get a real flavour of the island here are some ideas:

Business and relaxation go together in Cyprus

10
Ways To Be A Local

Adapt to Mediterranean time – go out late, eat late, don't rush and take everything as it comes.

Wear appropriate dress when you visit churches, monasteries and mosques – no shorts or bare shoulders.

Take an afternoon siesta to escape the hot summer sun. Retreat into the shade to sleep or spin out a relaxed lunch.

Browse the bazaars and weekly fruit and vegetable markets for unrivalled value and local colour.

Buy hand-made Lefkara lace and other embroidery work. Traditionally, a Cypriot bride had to have 100 sheets and pillowcases in her dowry – but you can start a collection with just one beautiful piece.

Order a strong coffee in a traditional village coffee-shop, sit back and watch the menfolk gossip and play cards and backgammon.

Linger over an alfresco dinner of *meze* dishes. With a range of over 30 items to choose from, you can try something different every night.

Buses and service taxis are a cheap and friendly alternative to rented cars and ordinary taxis.

Locals don't get drunk in public – you shouldn't either as they will be offended if you do.

Enjoy exotic butterflies such as the Cleopatra and the two-tailed pasha.

10
Good Places To Have Lunch

Mandra Tavern
✉ Dionysou Street, Kato Pafos ☎ 06 234129. Traditional kebabs.

Militzis Restaurant
✉ 42 Piyale Pasa, Larnaka ☎ 04 65567. Varied fare and first rate fish.

Napa Taverna
✉ Demokratias 15, Agía Napa ☎ 03 721280. One of the first taverns in Agía Napa and one of the best.

Phini Taverna
✉ Foini Village ☎ 05 421828. Traditional dishes and fresh trout in a mountain village.

Porto Lachi
✉ Seafront at Latsi ☎ 06 321529. Wonderful seafood in a splendid harbour setting.

Tsolias
✉ Coral Bay ☎ 06 621238. Marvellous headland situation overlooking the bay.

Panagiotis Taverna
✉ Governor's Beach, east of Limassol ☎ 05 637042. Simple food in a setting overlooking the sea, enhanced by Socratic musing from the proprietor.

Petra tou Romiou Restaurant and Fish Tavern
☎ 06 996005. Marvellous views over the celebrated rock. A short distance off the main road.

Set Fish Restaurant

✉ Kyrenia Harbour
☎ 08 152336. Good harbour position. Wide range of fresh fish every day. Good Kalamari.

Vangelis

✉ Located a little outside Paralimni on the Deryneia Road ☎ 03 821456. Popular with locals; for something different try the pigeon or rabbit

Top Activities

Sunbathing:
In Cyprus all the uncertainty is taken out of this demanding occupation, for the sun shines all day every day.

Sea: **Severe** – These days there are more ways of following a motor boat than standing upright on two planks of wood. A multitude of flexible inflatables, including the notorious banana, skim the waves during invigorating high speed tows. Some aficionados of the foam prefer jet skis, ideal for that useful adrenaline boost.

Sea: **Sedate** – These relaxing pastimes include airbed floating and the ever popular pedalos.

Swimming: Few can resist the warm turquoise sea. Free style here does not mean a fast crawl, every technique known to man, and some others, are performed with great virtuosity.

Luxuriating: Participants welcome the enervating heat and thus stimulated take their ease at poolside, on the terrace or the beach. Lunch does interfere but the consolation is that a good repast makes it that much easier to regress into the torpid state.

Parascending: Incredibly, people queue for this expensive death defying adventure. One nervous, critical bound and it is up into the thermals.

Golf: One has to admire the Cypriots – nothing is too daunting. In brown waterless landscapes they have created greens. Golf in Cyprus is still in its infancy, but who can doubt that it will be a huge success. (➤ 112)

Hill Walks: In summer it is very hot for walking. Nevertheless, several interesting trails have been laid out in the Akamas and the Troodos.

Diving: Explorations of the wonders of the deep are well catered for at the diving centres and some hotels around the island.

Horse riding: There are centres in Nicosia, Limassol and Pafos. Riding can be through the countryside, including the Troodos Mountains.

Cycling: There are scores of bicycles for hire in all the resorts. Main roads can be very busy at weekends and the tourist office advises cyclists to avoid them at this time.

Interesting Diversions

View the forbidden city of Famagusta through binoculars from the roof of an enterprising Greek Cypriot's house in Deryneia. There is a small charge.

Walk the Pediaios River in Nicosia. Join the river bed at the ford near the Presidential Palace and take a very unusual route into town. Not to be undertaken if rain is about, as a flash flood would be dangerous.

Walk the Green Line in the walled city of Nicosia. Greek and Turkish soldiers are almost eyeball to eyeball and the air is tense. Keep the camera out of sight.

Visit the Keo wine distillery in Limassol. 1 Franklin Roosevelt Avenue ☎ 05 362053.

Walk a gorge in the Akamas. Exalt Travel, Pafos ☎ 06 243803, will arrange a guided excursion.

Hire a pedalo or similar on Agía Napa beach and paddle through the unusual weathered rock formations at the east end of the bay.

Take a 2- or 3-day boat trip from Limassol to the Holy Land. Local travel agents will provide all details (try Louis Cruise Lines, Limassol ☎ 05 340000).

Visit the Grivas Museum on the beach near Chlorakas and see the wooden ship, *Ágios Georgios*, used for gun running during the EOKA campaign.

See the sunrise over the Kyrenian Mountains from the Mesaoria (central plain). Spectacular effects reward a spectacularly early start.

Watch the vultures on Besparmak (Pentadaktylos) mountain (east of Kyrenia). Drive to the pass and make the short walk in. Keep an eye open for adders.

A Drive Around Western Cyprus

Distance
120km

Time
3½–8 hours

Start/end point
Pafos town centre
✠ 57B2

Lunch
There are good restaurants in
Pano Panagia or fish
restaurants in Latsi (£ –££)

Follow the signs to Polis, heading out of Pafos, and after 15km turn right into the hills towards the village of Polemi.

The road runs through low hills cut into terraces to support the vines.

Some 20km after Polemi, the route reaches the village of Pano Panagia.

This is the birthplace of Archbishop Makarios (➤ 67). A further 1.5km uphill is Chrysorrogiatissa Monastery (➤ 62) which, at a height of 610m, commands some really good views of the surrounding area.

The drive then retraces the route to Pano Panagia and Asprogia, and turns right before Kannaviou on to a minor road to Fyti and Simou.

These are remote villages where traditional ways of life are still visible; do not be surprised to encounter donkeys at every turn. The villages are something of a maze, but almost all the streets lead back to the through road.

Turn northwest, rejoining the main Polis road at Loukrounou. From here it is a smooth drive down to Polis (➤ 67).

Slow but sure, who needs to hurry?

Polis has a choice of good beaches, either in the town itself, to the west in Latsi, or near the Baths of Aphrodite.

The return trip takes the western road out of Polis to the old hill village of Drouseia. The road then continues south through the hills, turning right at Kathikas, ending up at Pegeia.

This small village is famous for its springs.

Rejoin the main road at Coral Bay (➤ 63), from where it is a quick run back to Pafos.

PANO PANAGIA ★

The village of Pano Panagia is the place where Archbishop Makarios was born. Makarios played a key role in the campaign for independence from the British and he was the first President of Cyprus from Independence in 1960 until his death in 1977.

His parent's house in the village is now a museum. It consists of two rooms, with his parent's bed, assorted crockery and family photographs. If nothing else, the house shows that the Archbishop had a humble background. In the main square is a cultural centre, which displays more photographs and memorabilia from the President's later life.

☩ 28B2
✉ Pano Panagia village centre
🕐 Cultural Centre: Tue–Sun 9–1, 2–5; Makarios's House: daily 10–1, 2–6
🍴 Many cafés in village (£)
💰 Cultural Centre: free. Makarios's House: donation requested.

POLIS ★★

The town has traditionally been the destination for backpackers and other more unconventional travellers. Most of the main restaurants and shops are to be found around a pedestrianised square, with a number of rooms and apartments to rent close by. There is a good beach a short walk from the town centre with a campsite adjacent.

Just east of the town, but difficult to find, is the ancient site of Marion, which was founded in the 7th century BC and developed into one of the ten City Kingdoms of Cyprus.

☩ 28B2

POMOS AND TO THE EAST ★★

There are some wonderful quiet beaches along this section of coast, and when the road climbs up into the cliffs there are some amazing views. Just beyond Pomos Point is a small fishing harbour and sheltered beach. Kokkina is a Turkish village and is inaccessible. The road detours inland and then reaches Kato Pyrgos where there is another isolated beach. No further progress is possible owing to the Turkish military.

☩ 28B2
✉ 22km northwest of Polis
🍴 Café at Kato Pyrgos (£)
🚌 Limited bus service from Polis to Pomos, at 11, 2, 4, 6; Sat 11, 2:30, 4

A quiet beach is worth the exploration

Nicosia &
the High Troodos

In contrast to all the other major towns of Cyprus, Nicosia lies inland on the Mesaoria, or central plain. This location allowed the city to avoid the devastation wreaked on the coastal towns by Arab raiders. Here the plain is relatively narrow with the Kyrenian mountains to the north and the foothills of the Troodos approaching the city from the southwest.

The northern boundary is no arbitrary choice, but the Green Line that divides Cyprus and cuts through the heart of Nicosia. Visitors will find it a frontier they cannot cross, except at one point in Nicosia, and this privilege is reserved only for people in the south.

The other boundaries are somewhat less formidable. To the south is a splendid area of valleys and villages; Stavros in the west is a lonely forest station; Machairas Monastery and its surrounding hills make up the eastern extremity.

'The island has in its midst a fair city called Nicosia, which is the capital of the kingdom, well walled, with its fine gates, which are three.'

P JOAN LOPEZ
(1770)

Nicosia (Lefkoşa)

Nicosia is the capital of Cyprus and is a divided city. The border, known as the Green Line, separates the Greek and Turkish sectors of the island and runs through the middle of the city. The Greek side has all the hallmarks of a modern westernised place and is a thriving shopping and business centre, although with its ancient history still visible. The northern sector has a more dilapidated and eastern feel to it with narrower streets and old fashioned shops.

No man's territory, abandoned wasteland of the Green Line

Nicosia is always busy and is always hotter than the coast, so summer visitors should not plan too strenuous a programme. Fortunately, the main attractions can be found within the old city walls and can be explored on foot. The walls themselves, built by the Venetians, still dominate.

An extensive modernisation and refurbishment programme is underway in the old part of town. The pedestrianised Laïki Geitonia area is the most obvious result of that programme. It is a pleasant place to wander, with all the facilities a tourist could need, and leads into some of the older shopping streets.

There is less to see in northern Nicosia and the narrow streets make it easy to get lost. However, almost all roads eventually lead to the main sight, the Selimiye Mosque, once Santa Sophia Cathedral, the minarets of which dominate this part of town. There are a number of other mosques in the vicinity and a few small museums and, for the more adventurous the Turkish Baths.

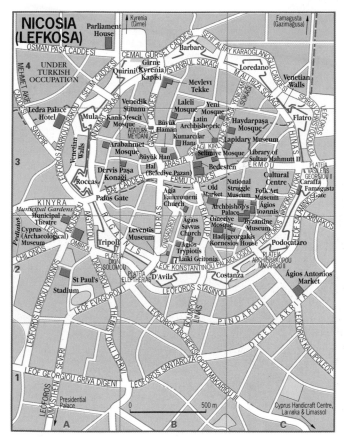

NICOSIA (LEFKOSA)

Parliament House

Kyrenia (Girne)

Famagusta (Gazimağusa)

UNDER TURKISH OCCUPATION

OSMAN PAŞA CADDESİ

CEMAL GURSEL CADDESI

Barbaro

SEHIT ALBAY KARAOGLANOGLU CADDESI

Girne

Quirini (Kyrenia) Kapisi

İSTANBUL SOKAGİ

Loredano

Venetian Walls

Mevlevi Tekke

Ledra Palace Hotel

Venedik Sütunu

Laleli Mosque

Yeni Mosque

Haydarpaşa Mosque

Flatro

Mula

Kanlı Mescit Mosque

Büyük Hamam

Latin Archbishopric

Lapidary Museum

Library of Sultan Mahmutt II

Arabahmet Mosque

ATATÜRK MEYDANI

Kumarcılar Hani

Selimiye Mosque

Derviş Paşa Konağı

Büyük Han

Bedesten

Cultural Centre

Hal (Belediye Pazarı)

ERMU

Caraffa

Roccas

Famagusta Gate

Pafos Gate

Agia Fancromeni Church

Old Market

National Struggle Museum

Folk Art Museum

KINYRA

Municipal Gardens

Municipal Theatre

Archbishop's Palace

Ágios Ioannis

Cyprus (Archaeological) Museum

Leventis Museum

Agios Savvas Church

Ömeriye Mosque

Byzantine Museum

Tripoli

Hadjigeorgakis Kornesios House

Podocátaro

Ágios Trypiotis

St Paul's

Laiki Geitonia

Stadium

D'Avila

Costanza

Ágios Antonios Market

Presidential Palace

Cyprus Handicraft Centre, Larnaka & Limassol

0   500 m

What to See in Greek Nicosia

ÁGIOS IOANNIS CATHEDRAL ★★

The cathedral lies within the Archbishopric and was built in 1662 on the site of an earlier Benedictine abbey church. It contains some fine, recently restored, 18th-century wall paintings and is ornately decorated throughout. It is claimed that it contained the finger of St John the Baptist until it was stolen by Mameluke raiders. The cathedral, now used for all official religious occasions, is smaller than one might expect of a building of such great importance, and is best visited early before the crowds arrive.

✚ 71C3
✉ Archbishopric
🕐 Mon–Sat 8–12, 2–4
🍴 Cafés near by (£)
♿ Free

71C2
Archbishopric
Mon–Fri 9–1, 2–5, Sat 9–1
Cafés near by (£)
Moderate

ARCHBISHOP MAKARIOS CULTURAL CENTRE (BYZANTINE MUSEUM)

The most important exhibits in the museum are the 6th-century Kanakaria Mosaics which were thought lost when they were stolen from their church on the Karpas peninsula in northern Cyprus. They were recovered when offered for sale on the international art market and were returned to this purpose-built wing of the museum. Also on show here are a large number of icons from churches around the island.

71A2
Museum Street
02 302189
Mon–Sat 9–5, Sun 10–1.
Closed 1 Jan, 25 Dec, Greek Orthodox Easter Sun
Café opposite (££)
Moderate

CYPRUS MUSEUM

The museum houses most of the important finds from sites across Cyprus – neolithic artefacts, Bronze-Age vases and clay figurines, Mycenaean objects from Kourion and some surprisingly sophisticated pottery. Two thousand figurines found at Agia Irini are displayed as they were found, gathered around a single altar. A wide range of sculptures are on show, as well as a huge bronze statue of Emperor Septimius and the famous green-horned god from Enkomi. There are impressive artefacts from Salamis, some mosaics and a reconstruction of a rock cut tomb.

71C3
Leoforus Athinon
Mon–Fri 10–1, 4–7, (5–8 Jul–Aug)
Cafés near by (£)
Free

FAMAGUSTA GATE

This was once the major entrance into the old city from the south and east. It is set into the old walls and has been restored to house a cultural centre which is used for exhibitions and other events. The whole area is now attracting artists who have set up studios in many of the old buildings.

71C2
Patriarchou Georgiou Street
02 302477
Mon–Fri 8–2, Sat 9–1
Cafés near by (£)
Cheap

HADJIGEORGAKIS KORNESIOS HOUSE (ETHNOGRAPHICAL MUSEUM)

This house belonged to the Great Dragoman of Cyprus, Hadjigeorgakis, at the end of the 18th century. The Dragoman was a translator, an important and powerful role at that period. The museum contains a number of inter-esting artefacts from the Dragoman's life, displayed in reconstructions of some of the original rooms, along with letters and documentation prepared by Hadjigeorgakis.

A Walk Around Nicosia

Start at Laïki Geitonia (➤ 74), the pedestrianised shopping area, and find Ippocratous Street immediately to the north.

Walk west and pass the Leventis Museum (➤ 74) to turn right into Onasagorou Street. In 250m there is an awkward junction, but generally proceed straight on down Mouson Street, after a slight move to the right. Continue for about 100m before turning right at the junction where there is a school on the corner. This is Lefkonos Street, and it crosses Aischylou Street, leading into Trikoupi Street. Turn right for 200m to reach Tylliria Square.

The Omerye Mosque lies directly ahead (➤ 74), and a short distance to the east down Patriarchos Gregorios Street is the Hadjigeorjakis House (➤ 72).

From the house it is 50m to the left turn into Zinonos Kitieos Street.

At the far end of this road is the Archbishop's Palace, a large, mock Venetian style building with a huge statue of Archbishop Makarios outside. The Byzantine Museum (➤ 71) and Agios Ioannis Cathedral are just beyond the palace on the left (➤ 72).

Continue northward into a pedestrianised area, down Agiou Ioannou Street to turn right and soon left along Antigonou Street. There is a mosque ahead. Turn right on to Ammochostou Street.

At the far end is Famagusta Gate (➤ 72) and it is then possible to follow the road around the Venetian Walls (➤ 86). There are some pleasant, well-watered gardens within the moat guarding the walls.

The main road then leads back to Laïki Geitonia, passing the Costanza Bastion, where the Byraktar Mosque can be seen.

Distance
3km

Time
2–4 hours

Start/end point
Laïki Geitonia
✚ 71B2
🚌 152 from Limassol/Pafos, 146 from Larnaka stop at Plateia Dionysios Solomou bus station just outside the walls

Lunch
There are many restaurants in the Laïki Geitonia area (£)

71B2

Within old city walls, northeast of Eleftheria Square

Many cafés (££)

LAÏKI GEITONIA

This is a pedestrianised area of old Nicosia where traditional old buildings have been restored, shops refurbished and trees planted. It is specifically aimed at the tourist, with a whole range of restaurants, handicraft shops and the tourist office as well as a small jewellery museum.

The old shopping streets of Ledra and Onasagoras which lead out of the Laïki Geitonia area are also interesting places to wander. Some more traditional shops can be found on these streets and at their northern end are the sandbags which mark the Green Line.

71B2

Ippokratous Street

02 451475

Tue–Sun 10–4:30. Closed 1 Jan, 25 Dec, Greek Orthodox Easter Sun

Café in basement (££)

Free

LEVENTIS MUSEUM

This museum, in the Laïki Geitonia area, is well set out and modest in size. Medieval finds are in the basement, some of which were uncovered when the building was being restored. The first floor deals with the period 2300 BC to the Turkish period and the ground floor covers the British colonial time as well as the city's more modern history. The documentation from this later period is particularly interesting although the commentaries can be a little partisan.

71B2

Trikoupi Street

Mon–Sat 10–12:30, 1:30–3:30

Cafés near by (£)

Free

ÖMERIYE MOSQUE ✪

As with many of the city's mosques, this building was originally a church and was converted in 1571 by Mustafa Paşa, the occupying Turkish General. He believed that the visit of the Muslim prophet Omar should be commemorated. As a result, the minaret was added and the old Lusignan tombstones used to cover the floor. The mosque is still used as a place of worship, but the public can climb the minaret, which offers splendid views of the city.

Did you know ?

The Ledra Palace Hotel used to be the main luxury hotel in Nicosia. It now stands on the Green Line, the home to British United Nations troops and is still marked with bullet holes from the 1974 conflict. It is used for meetings between the two sides both official and unofficial.

WALLED CITY (➤ 23, TOP TEN)

What to See in Turkish Nicosia

BÜYÜK HAMAN ✪

This was once the Church of St George, built in the 14th century and subsequently converted to a baths by the Turks. The main room is domed, the floor well below street level. On Fridays it is women only, other days men only. Should it be locked the café owner on the west side has the key.

71B3
Mousa Orfenbey Sokagi
Jun–Sep, daily 7:30–1, 4–6; Oct–May, daily 8–1, 2–6
Café next door (£)
Free entry; baths: moderate

BÜYÜK HAN ✪✪

The building was commissioned in 1572 by Mustafa Paşa, the first Ottoman governor of Cyprus. It was a simple hotel, complete with stables and a wonderful little mosque in the courtyard. Perhaps the nadir of its fortunes was when it became Nicosia's central prison in 1893.

Its days of neglect are now over – the Department of Antiquities are restoring it, albeit as a museum.

71B3
Arasta Sokagi
Not yet open to the public

LAPIDARY MUSEUM ✪

The building is on two levels, perhaps once the home of a wealthy Venetian family. Assorted wooden relics from mosques and churches display very fine carving.

In the courtyard is a random selection of Corinthian capitals, carved stone heads and a section of a beautifully designed rose window.

71C3
Northeast of the Selimiye Mosque
Jun–Sep, daily 7.30–2, 4–6; Oct–May 8–1, 2–5. If locked, try custodian at the Library of Sultan Mahmut II across the road
Free

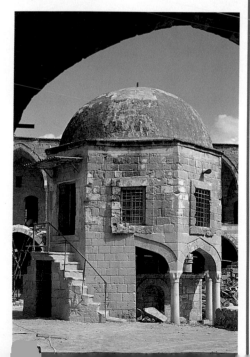

Büyük Han's little mosque, awaiting restoration to its former splendour

75

⊞ 71B4
✉ Girne Caddesi
🕐 Jun–Sep, Mon–Fri
7:30–2; Oct–May 9–1,
2–4:45
🖐 Cheap

MEVLEVI TEKKE
(ETHNOGRAPHICAL MUSEUM)
✪✪✪

This was the home of the whirling Dervishes, a sect founded in the 13th century. The rooms have a simple elegance, complete with a splendid minstrels' gallery looking down on where the Dervishes, heads lowered in contemplation, would stretch out their arms and spin at ever increasing speed. In 1925 Kemal Attaturk forbade the dancing in an attempt to modernise Turkish culture. After 20 years the ruling was relaxed and the dance celebrated once more. To one side is an interesting collection of costumes, wedding dresses and musical instruments. Adjoining is a long mausoleum of 15 tombs, resting places of important Dervishes.

Sixteen Dervishes would perform the dance and one can almost feel their presence today

⊞ 71B3
✉ Selimiye Sokagi
🕐 Daily
🖐 Free

SELIMIYE MOSQUE
✪✪✪

This impressive building was a Christian masterpiece before becoming a mosque of the Ottoman Turks, the most important in Cyprus. The elevations of magnificent windows, portals and buttresses are worryingly discordant, the reason – the soaring minarets. They are notable landmarks in the walled city, and their imposition on the west front by the Turks reflects the momentous events of 1570–1 when the Turks subjugated the city.

The original cathedral was started in 1209 and substantially completed 117 years later. In reality it was never quite finished, work carrying on long after the consecration.

Everything changed with the arrival of the Turks. All the Christian decoration of the cathedral was destroyed. Soon after, work was started on the minarets and the building became the cathedral of Santa Sophia until the name was changed to the Selimiye Mosque in 1954.

What to See in the High Troodos

ÁGIOS IRAKLEIDIOS ⭐

The monastery was founded in the Byzantine era, and it is dedicated to the saint who guided St Paul and St Barnabas to nearby Tamassos during their missionary travels. St Irakleidios lived in a cave, and the first church was built around it. His skull is kept in the present building in a silver case, and many believe it has miraculous powers to heal the sick.

The complex is now a convent. It dates from 1773 and is a simple construction of good appearance, enhanced by excellent gardens. These are meticulously tended by the nuns and in summer are an oasis of greenery and colour in the barren landscape.

🕂 28C2
✉ Near the village of Politikon
🕓 Daily
🍴 Café opposite (£)
🖐 Free

ASINOU CHURCH (PANAGIA FORVIOTISSA) ⭐⭐

The fame of this church is such that it is quite a surprise to find it so tiny, hidden away on a north-facing hillside of eucalyptus and pine trees. A steep clay-tiled outer roof protects the vulnerable Byzantine dome and treasures within.

Asinou remains unscathed in 900 years. The frescoes are the best of Cyprus's painted churches, the earliest dating back to the 12th century. They were added to over the years and culminate in the powerful examples carried out by refugee painters from Asia Minor.

Christ is depicted in the sanctuary and the dome of the narthex, gazing sternly down. All around the rank and file are beautifully illustrated.

🕂 28C2
✉ Near Nikitari
🕓 Ask in Nikitari for the priest with the key
🖐 Free

Ornate interior of Ágios Irakleidios

Religion is alive and well in Cyprus; a new church at Kakopetria

> ### *Did you know ?*
>
> *In the 15th century the Venetians built a series of bridges over the rivers that cut into the Troodos Mountains. They were for pack animals, particularly camels, to carry copper ore from Mylikouri, Kaminaria, and Foini, high in the hills to Pafos for export.*
> *Alas the camel has gone the way of the export trade. The last census in 1965 counted only 90. Today there is perhaps one, or possibly two, giving rides to holidaymakers in Pafos.*

 28C2
 Tue–Sat 9–4, Sun 11–4
Several cafés (£–££)
Free

KAKOPETRIA ✪

The village stands high in the poplar lined Solea Valley. As the hill villages go, it is quite large and a favourite holiday resort of the Cypriots. They come mainly in the summer to see relatives or to escape the suffocating lowland heat. As a consequence, there are several small hotels and restaurants. It is certainly not a smart looking place, the buildings are generally old or ramshackle or both, but it has charm.

Three kilometres up the valley is the celebrated church of Ágios Nikolaos tis Stegis with its famous roof. Below the town, at Galata, are the tiny churches of Panagia Eleousa and Panagia Theotokos, looking like country barns, with their roofs nearly to the ground.

KYKKOS MONASTERY (► 20, TOP TEN)

A Drive into The Troodos

For Pafos visitors, the drive proper starts 17km towards Limassol – the left turn at the Xeros River for Nikokleia, Mamonia and Agios Georgios must be taken. It is a slow and splendid 55km up to Platres (Pano), through orchards and farmland.

The route from Limassol begins about 13km to the west, immediately after Erimi – the road right to Kantou, Souni and Agios Amvrosios is the one to take. About 37km of pleasant uphill driving leads to Omodos village, once charming and now a popular tourist attraction. It is another 14km to meet up with the Pafos travellers at Platres.

Distance
Limassol – 200km
Pafos – 220km

Time
5–8 hours

Start/end point
Limassol or Pafos
✚ 28B1

Lunch
Caruralli
✉ Pedoulas
☎ 02 952441

Traverse the confusing streets of Platres to reach the main Nicosia–Limassol highway and go left up to Troodos village – about 7km. The route runs for 11km along the minor road to Prodromos.

This is the highest village in Cyprus, and an early short detour to Mount Olympus (▶ 80) can be made if time permits.

Soon after Prodromos, the descent of the north slopes of Olympus becomes quite dramatic in places, as the road twists and turns above the abyss.

This is a cherry-growing area, and its main villages – Pedoulas, Moutoullas and Kalopanagiotis – are reached in regular succession. Moutoullas is also famous for its spring water.

After the excitement of the hairpin bends, it is a simple run of about 8km before sweeping east towards Linou and the Limassol–Nicosia highway.

Omodos's main street may have lost some of its character but not its sleepy afternoons

The return leg is straightforward. Turn right for Troodos/Limassol and climb the mountain. Kakopetria, after 14km, is worth the short detour.
At Troodos village, Limassol-bound travellers simply continue for about 55km, via Trimiklini and Pano Polemedia. Pafos-bound drivers can turn off at Platres to reverse their route via Mandria, Agios Nikolaos and Mamonia.

MACHAIRAS MONASTERY ✪✪

28C2
Near Fikardou, eastern Troodos
Daily
Cafés near by (£)
Free

The Monastery was founded in the 12th century, and grew around an icon of the Virgin Mary, but successive fires destroyed the original church and its wall paintings and in 1892 the entire monastery was burnt to the ground.

The present building dates from the early 20th century, and its elevations are unusual, fortress like, and broken up with wooden balconies. Within is an impressive iconostasis, illuminated by chandeliers. On feast days rituals take place starting early and culminating at midnight with the abbot emerging with the holy fire, a glowing candle.

The simple interior of the monastery is in contrast to its unusual external elevations

Outside a track leads down the wooded valley to the cave of Grigoris Afxentiou, second in command of EOKA during the uprising against the British. In 1957 a shepherd betrayed him and British soldiers surrounded the cave entrance. Afxentiou chose to fight, dying eight hours later in his hideout.

MOUNT OLYMPUS ✪

28B2
55km from Limassol, 97km from Nicosia
Cafés in Troodos village 4km away (£)

At 1,951m above sea level, the summit of Mount Olympus is the highest ground in Cyprus. It is not an inaccessible peak, as a narrow road winds all the way to the top, stopping at the unappealing collection of radar domes. As a mountain, it is thereby compromised, nevertheless it is worth the journey simply to gaze out over Cyprus, the land falling away all around.

This magnificent view is even better in winter. It is an unforgettable experience to stand in deep snow, bathed in sunlight, and look over to Morfou Bay and on to the Taurus Mountains of Turkey.

Dawn over Troodos, splendid but deceptively cold; temperatures on high ground are close to freezing

> ## *Did you know ?*
>
> *The adverse fortune of recent years of one of Cyprus's oldest, shyest and most distinctive residents is now over. The moufflon, the largest wild animal in Cyprus, was declared a protected species in 1995. This deliverance was timely – the numbers of the impressive horned sheep had been reduced to just 300 by relentless hunting.*

PANAGIA TOU ARAKA

The paintings in this church are marvellous. Unfortunately the drive to get there is long and tiring, albeit through superb scenery. To confound matters, the church is generally locked, admission being by courtesy of the priest normally found in the village of Lagoudera.

The church retains the most complete series of wall paintings of the Byzantine period on the island and they were recently cleaned, courtesy of UNESCO. They represent the metropolitan classicizing school in full bloom. Even visitors who know little of style, technique and iconography will surely appreciate their magnificence.

✪

🕂 28C2
✉ Lagoudera
🕐 Sun and courtesy of the priest in Lagoudera
🍴 Café in nearby village (£)
 Free

The North

This is the Turkish-controlled part of Cyprus, underpopulated compared to the remainder of the island, where change is slow in coming, perhaps due to the easy-going temperament of the Turkish Cypriot but certainly attributable in part to the embargoes imposed by most of the world.

Whatever the objectives of these impositions, they cannot detract from the magnificent scenery, and they have certainly prevented destructive mass tourism.

Along the north shore the spectacular Kyrenian Mountains run unbroken for 90km. To the south the land is flat, opening out into the Mesaoria east of Nicosia. In summer it is impressively barren; in spring the colour has to be seen to be believed.

The fabled Karpasia is spectacular with the blue Mediterranean visible to north and south of the narrow peninsula .

'Cyprus is the farthest of the Christian lands. All ships and all wares... must needs come first to Famagusta and pilgrims from every land journeying to countries over sea must touch at Cyprus.'

C D COBHAM
Excerpta Cypria

Famagusta (Gazimağusa)

The city is divided, although not between Greek and Turk. Varosha, the new town, with its painted hotels bordering the sandy beach, is closed to all but the military. It has been so since 1974. Visitors must therefore concentrate on the walled city. They are adequately compensated in that it is one of the finest surviving examples of medieval military architecture in existence.

The fruit stall's crude awning is an essential protection against the searing midday heat

To pass through the massive walls is to pass through history, from the time of the Lusignans, Genoese and Venetians to the bloody siege by the Turks in 1570. They stormed the walls and all Cyprus was theirs for over 300 years, and the scene was set for the troubles of today.

In the narrow streets the shops are unchanged by time or fashion. Dark interiors hide a miscellany of goods. The town can be a bustling place of noise and activity, but more often it is calm, the residents going about their business in a relaxed manner. They may not be as outgoing as their Greek Cypriot countrymen in the south, but they are equally courteous and helpful.

There is much unexpected open space in all directions; a chaotic panorama of unkempt gardens and scrubland where palm trees shade ancient domed churches. Splendid crumbling examples of medieval buildings are all around. The battered minaret and massive buttress of Lala Mustafa Paşa mosque are an impressive landmark for any who get lost in these exotic surroundings.

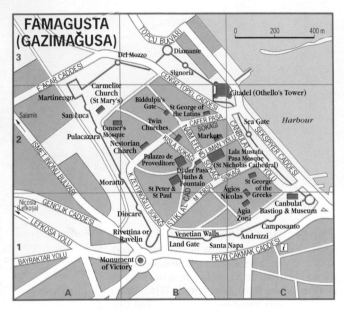

FAMAGUSTA
(GAZIMAĞUSA)

0   200   400 m

TOPÇU BULVARI

Del Mozzo   Diamante

Signoria

F. AÇAR CADDESI

CENGIZ TOPEL CADDESI

Carmelite
Church
(St Mary's)

Martinengo

Biddulph's
Gate

Citadel (Othello's Tower)

St George of
the Latins

CAFER PAŞA
SOKAĞI

Salamis

San Luca

Tanner's
Mosque

Twin
Churches

Sea Gate   Harbour

Pulacazara

NAIM EFENDI SOKAĞI

LIMAN YOLU

CANBULAT

SEKSPIYER CADDESI

ISMET INÖNÜ BULVARI

Nestorian
Church

KISLA SOKAĞI

Lala Mustafa
Paşa Mosque
(St Nicholas Cathedral)

Palazzo de
Proveditore

Djafer Paşa
Baths &
Fountain

M. ERSU SOKAĞI

YOLU

Moratto

St Peter &
St Paul

Ágios
Nicolas

St George
of the
Greeks

K. ZEYTINOĞLU SOKAĞI

ISTIKLAL CAD.

M. ERSU

Agia
Zoni

Canbulat
Bastion & Museum

Nicosia
(Lefkoşa)

GENÇLIK CADDESI

Diocare

Camposanto

LEFKOŞA YOLU

Rivettina or
Ravelin

Venetian Walls

Andruzzi

Land Gate   Santa Napa

BAYRAKTAR YOLU

Monument
of Victory

FEVZI ÇAKMAK CADDESI

A   B   C

1   2   3

What to See in Famagusta

LALA MUSTAFA PAŞA MOSQUE   ✪✪✪

The building has been a mosque for over 400 years, but, the architecture is of a Latin cathedral. There is a single minaret, well executed but certainly out of place. Even so, it is still possible to admire the splendid six-light window of the west front. Three portals lead to the impressive interior, where Moslem simplicity has enabled the fine Gothic nave to survive the loss of its Christian decoration.

Lala Mustafa was the victorious commander of the Ottoman Turks when they broke into Famagusta in 1571. Surprisingly, the mosque only received his name in 1954, before which it was called the Mosque of Santa Sophia.

ST GEORGE OF THE GREEKS   ✪

This is a substantial church, if deteriorating significantly. It was built in 1359, probably in opposition to the Latin Cathedral of St Nicholas (now Lala Mustafa Paşa Mosque). The three apses are traditionally semicircular. A dome covered the middle section of the church, but by all accounts it collapsed under cannon fire in 1571. Some wall paintings survive, the best being in the eastern apse.

✚ 84B2
✉ Naim Efendi Sokaği
🕐 Daily
🍴 Café opposite west front
(£)
♿ Free

✚ 84C2
✉ Mustafa Ersu Sokaği
🕐 Daily
♿ Free

84

A Famagusta Walk

The walk starts at the Land Gate entrance of the historic walled city.

Istiklal Caddesi is directly opposite and should be followed, taking care not to lose it at the three-way junction after 130m.

About 130m further, on the left, is the Church of SS Peter and Paul (► 86), now a public library.

A right turn along Sinan Paşa Sokagi leads to the Palazzo de Proveditore (Venetian Palace).

From here it is a small distance to Namik Kemal Zindani (Square), overlooked by the magnificent west front of Lala Mustafa Paşa Mosque (► 84).

A short retreat (to the west) picks up Kisla Sokagi, and in 130m are the twin churches (now restored) of the Knights Templar and Knights Hospitaller. Immediately beyond the churches the road turns right, to the northeast, and in 120m Cafer Paşa Sokagi.

At the eastern end stand the ruined, but impressive buttresses and lancet windows of St George of the Latins. The Citadel (Othello's Tower) is a short distance to the north and should not be bypassed.

The walk continues alongside the sea wall, down Canbulat Yolu, to reach the splendid Sea Gate after 200m.

In another 160m, a short detour along M Ersu Sokagi brings walkers to the substantial Church of St George of the Greeks (► 84). Returning to the main road, the Canbulat Museum is reached in 300m.

The return to the Land Gate is about 1100m. Pass outside the walls at the Canbulat Museum and follow the south wall.

Distance
2.75km

Time
1–3½ hours

Start/end point
Land Gate
✚ 84B1

Lunch
Café opposite west front of Lala Mustafa Paşa Mosque (£)

Land Gate and Ravelin, scene of desperate fighting in the great siege of 1570–1

85

84B2

✉ Abdullah Pasa Sokagi

🕐 Mon–Fri 7:30–2;
Oct–May 8–1, 2–5

🍴 Cafés near by (£)

✋ Free

84B1

🕐 Citadel and museum:
Jun–Sep 9–1:30,
4:30–6:30; Oct–May,
8–1, 2:30–5. Elsewhere
no restrictions

🍴 Cafés near by (£)

✋ Citadel and museum:
cheap; elsewhere free

---

*A Venetian winged lion
guards the entrance to
the Citadel, or Othello's
Tower*

ST PETER AND ST PAUL (SINAN PAŞA MOSQUE)

The Latin church is distinctive with its spectacular flying buttresses. It was once used as a mosque, as the ruined minaret in one corner testifies, but today it is the municipal library. At other times it stored potatoes and grain and was known as the wheat mosque. On entering, the reason for the massive buttresses is apparent – the nave is of tremendous height, exerting a colossal force on the outside walls.

VENETIAN WALLS ✪✪✪

The original plan of the town was laid out by the Lusignans, but, when the Venetians took over in 1489 they completely renovated the boundary walls. Experts in military architecture, they lowered the ramparts but increased the thickness, taking out all features that were vulnerable to cannon fire.

Any tour of the fortifications should take into account the great heat of summer and the unguarded parapets everywhere.

The Citadel should be visited. It is also known as Othello's Tower, a name derived from Shakespeare's play, set in a 'seaport in Cyprus.' Four great cylindrical towers guard the corners of the Citadel. Over the entrance the carving is an impressive winged lion of St Mark. The great hall is a massive vaulted chamber.

Taking a clockwise circuit of the walls, the Sea Gate, 200m southeast, is the next place of interest. The gate's portcullis is part of the original Venetian installation.

In another 500m is the Canbulat Gate and bastion (Canbulat was a Turkish hero of the siege), now a museum. Muskets and swords are displayed next to period dresses finished with fine embroidery.

Three bastions on the southern wall lead to the Land Gate, the main entrance to the town. It is part of the Ravelin, a bastion considered impregnable when built, but later found wanting as its ditch offered cover to the enemy.

KYRENIA (GIRNE) ✪✪✪

Kyrenia is unmatched in the rest of Cyprus. This eulogy attributes nothing to Kyrenia town and environs. It is all to do with the harbour and its magnificent setting. Certainly the old buildings of the quayside, with the exception of the customs houses, have all been reconstituted as restaurants and bars, nevertheless, everything seems just perfect, day or night.

A huge cylindrical bastion from Venetian times forms the east end of the harbour, a minaret rises up in the middle ground and an Anglican spire in the west. Mountain ridges and summits run unbroken into the hazy distance.

28C3
Several cafés around the harbour (£–££)

Empty tables on Kyrenia's lovely waterfront, a rare phenomena

CASTLE ✪✪✪

The origins of the castle are Lusignan, but it was the Venetians who made it impregnable. Inside, sunlight streams down from hidden windows and openings. Entry into the complex structure is over the moat, now dry, to reach a gatehouse. Progress is then up a ramp, passing a small Byzantine chapel and then on to the northwest tower. Here is the tomb of Sadik Paşa, killed in 1570, during the Turkish conquest of Cyprus.

Various routes can be taken to complete a tour of the castle, care being needed to keep clear of the unguarded battlements and drops.

There is much of interest, but the shipwreck museum should not be missed. It houses the oldest ship ever raised from the seabed. The blackened hulk, astonishingly well preserved, is no less than 2,300 years old. It was lifted from the sea in 1968–9.

28C3
Harbourside
Jun–Sep, daily 9–7; Oct–May, 9–1, 2–4:45
Cheap

What to See in The North

BELLAPAIS ABBEY ✪✪✪

The location of the abbey on the northern slopes of the Kyrenia Hills is marvellous. Far below are the almond and olive groves of the fertile coastal plain with Kyrenia in miniature to the west.

Augustinian canons founded the abbey at the end of the 12th century, its importance lasting for some 300 years, but substantial parts collapsed long ago. The cloister is half ruined, flamboyant tracery hangs down from the pointed arches.

On the north side is the Refectory, where the vaults of the roof appear to spring lightly from their capitals. Six tall windows look out on to the northern shore, and an exquisite pulpit, reached by an intricate stair, is ingeniously built into the thickness of the wall.

The 13th-century church is generally locked, but the custodian may open it on request.

In 1995 forest fires swept through the Kyrenian Mountains, advancing rapidly on Beylerbeyi, the village where the author Lawrence Durrell lived from 1953–6. In his celebrated *Bitter Lemons* he had written 'two things spread quickly; gossip and a forest fire'. It was only good fortune and the skill of the fire-fighters that prevented the destruction of Beylerbeyi in July 1995.

The abbey church, the oldest and best preserved part, is occasionally used for services

Did you know ?

Lawrence Durrell passed some of his leisure time drinking coffee and telling stories under the Tree of Idleness in Beylerbeyi (Bellapais). He warned against this relaxation if work remained to be done. Two adjoining cafés now lay claim to the tree, to the amusement of Sabri Tahir, who sold his village house to Durrell. He considers they are arguing over the wrong tree.

A Drive from Kyrenia to Kantara

The outward leg of this drive has few route-finding problems, staying close to the magnificent shore most of the way.

Drivers should take the coast road east out of Kyrenia, towards Agios Epiktitos (Çatalköy).

In colonial days the British put down mile posts and all beaches of significance on this north shore were described by the distance to Kyrenia. Six Mile Beach (also Acapulco), Eight Mile Beach and Twelve Mile Beach are all on the route. The latter is the longest sandy stretch on the coast, but it cannot be seen from the road. The villages of Karaagac, Esentepe, Bahceli and Tatlisu are all 2 or 3km off the main route. A detour to Tatlisu is recommended.

From the Tatlisu junction it is another 19km to reach the south turn to Kaplica. Now the road climbs steeply up to the village of Kantara.

Its castle (► 90), another 6km along the mountain ridge, is certainly worth visiting.

Return to the village, before starting the rapid descent to Turnalar, Yarkoy and on to the pleasant village of Bogaz, overlooking the Bay of Famagusta. The return section of the drive is southwest for 4km, before turning west to Iskele, the birthplace of Grivas, the EOKA leader.

Gecitkale, a large village, in a parched landscape in summer, is another 19km. The narrow road runs due west past a collection of rather poor looking villages.

Beycoy and Degirmenlik can be confusing – get there before sunset, and take the road to Kyrenia. It ascends rapidly to the pass at 750m above sea level, with Besparmak Mountain looming large to the right.

Now it is all downhill towards the sea, with another 12km along the coast to Kyrenia.

Take a well-earned driving rest at a harbourside café.

Distance
190km

Time
4½–7½ hours

Start/end point
Kyrenia
✚ 28C3

Lunch
Cafés in Kantara village (£)

⊞ 29E3
✉ Near Kantara village
◷ Daily
🍴 Cafés in Kantara village (£)
🖑 Free

KANTARA ✪✪

Kantara is the most easterly of the great Lusignan fortresses of the northern shore. At 600m above sea level, its ramparts crown rocky crags, with the north shore way below and stretching into the distance. The location at the eastern end of the mountain range gave the garrison control of the Karpasia peninsula. Visitors can, in a brief visual journey, survey this unique land formation in its entirety.

Most of the castle is a ruin, although the formidable outer wall is substantially intact. Entrance is gained through a ruined barbican and two towers. Steps lead on to vaulted chambers and medieval toilets. On the highest ground, only a Gothic window remains.

ST HILARION CASTLE (► 24, TOP TEN)

SALAMIS (► 25, TOP TEN)

⊞ 28B2
✉ Near Gemikonagi
◷ Open access
🖑 Cheap

SOLI ✪✪

The founders of Soli came from Greece and they created a city destined to play a major role in the struggle against Persian rule in the 5th and 4th centuries BC. However, only the work of the later Romans survives. They cut a theatre out of a rocky hillside overlooking Morfou Bay. Today, most of this substantial work is a reconstruction. Near the road are the remains of a colonnade leading to an agora. Some mosaics survive, the bird representations being most impressive.

The wealth of Soli lay with its copper, mined from the surrounding hills. Boats from the city's harbour, long silted up, carried the metal to many parts of the Mediterranean.

⊞ 28B3
✉ Near Gemikonagi
◷ Open access
🖑 Moderate

VOUNI ✪✪

The road to ruined Vouni palace spirals spectacularly upwards, a splendid area where the Troodos Mountains meet the northern shore. A series of terraces, swept bare by time, climb the hillside. The palace was clearly a substantial construction, with apartments, baths and court-yards. Little is known but it was built in the 5th century BC by a pro-Persian king from Marion; possibly to counter the power of nearby Soli, a city loyal to the Greeks. The rooms for bathing have a water system comparable to those of the Romans, but it is centuries earlier. At the top of the hill are the ruins of the Greek-style Temple of Athena.

Where To...

Larnaka & the Southeast

Prices
Prices are approximate, based on a three-course meal for one, without drinks and service:

Republic of Cyprus
£ = up to C£7
££ = C£7–C£14
£££ = over C£14

Northern Cyprus
£ = up to TL1,800000
££ = TL1,800000–TL3,600000
£££ = over TL3,600000

Agía Napa

Le Bistro d' Hier (££)
Menu changes daily. French selection. Vegetarian food on request.
✉ **11 Odyseos Elitis Street,** ☎ **03 721838** ⏰ **Daily until late**

Georgis Flambé (£)
Tourist menu in al fresco surroundings.
✉ **9 Ippocratou Street** ☎ **03 7211504** ⏰ **Daily until late. Closed in winter**

Oleander Taverna (££)
One of the oldest establishments in the resort. It has a reputation for good varied food and service.
✉ **Agía Napa** ☎ **03 721951** ⏰ **Daily**

Villa Fioria (£££)
Italian menu prepared to a high standard.
✉ **Kryou Street** ☎ **No tel** ⏰ **Daily**

VIPs (££)
International cuisine, charcoal grills and some excellent Cypriot specialities. Vegetarian dishes on request.
✉ **Napa Star Hotel, Makarios Avenue** ☎ **03 721540 ext 3027** ⏰ **Daily until late**

Larnaka

La Gourmandise (£££)
High class French cuisine.
✉ **Dhekalia Road** ☎ **04 624100** ⏰ **Daily**

Megalos Pefkos (££)
The location is good, right on the shore by the fort. Fresh fish, Cyprus *meze* and steaks, plus a free drink. Vegetarian choice.
✉ **Ankara Street** ☎ **04 628566** ⏰ **Daily until late**

Monte Carlo (££)
Overlooking the bay with a nice line in traditional Cypriot dishes, *meze* a speciality. Stylishly decorated place with a balcony.
✉ **28 Piale Pashia Street** ☎ **04 653815** ⏰ **Daily**

1900 Art Café (£)
Very good local cuisine in an attractively restored old house.
✉ **Stassinou 6** ☎ **04 653027** ⏰ **Daily 9–2, 6–12**

Rendez Vous Creperie (££)
The fondue is served here is just as good as the pancakes.
✉ **Dhekalia Road** ☎ **04 644532** ⏰ **Daily for dinner, Closed Tue, Oct–May**

Roast Inn (££)
Carvery bar and *à la carte* British Sunday lunch.
✉ **Dhekalia Road (Palm Beach Hotel area)** ☎ **04 644966 or 724015** ⏰ **Apr–Oct: daily 6–10; Nov–Mar: Tue–Sat 6–10, Sun 2–10**

Tudor Inn (££)
Steaks served in a variety of ways with excellent sauces. Vegetarian dishes are also available.
✉ **28a Lala Mustafa, Larnaka** ☎ **04 625608** ⏰ **Daily**

Vassos Varoshiotis (££)
Specialises in fish.
✉ **Piale Pashia 7** ☎ **04 655865** ⏰ **Daily**

Protaras

Anemos Beach Restaurant (£)
Good value food served in this taverna in busy seaside resort.
✉ **Fig Tree Bay** ☎ **03 831488** ⏰ **Daily**

Limassol & the South

Avdimou

Melanda Taverna (£)
A good place to have lunch, right by the golden sands.
✉ Avdimou Beach 🕓 Daily

Limassol

Assos Restaurant (££)
A wide range of Cypriot and international dishes.
✉ Amathountos Avenue, Amathus ☎ 05 321945
🕓 Daily

Blue Island (££)
Excellent *meze*, but good in all respects. Rightly popular with Limassol's well-to-do.
✉ Amathountas Avenue, Amathous ☎ 05 321466

Floyiera (££)
Good food and occasional live music.
✉ Patron 25, Germasogeia ☎ 05 325751 🕓 Daily

Glaros Taverna (££)
Taverna in prime setting above the water's edge serving good fish *meze*, cuttlefish in red wine a speciality.
✉ Agiou Antoniou 36 ☎ 05 357046 🕓 Lunch, dinner. Closed Sat, Sun dinner

Lefteris Tavern (££)
Special *meze* and village wine come with Cypriot hospitality in an old style building. Vegetarian dishes can be provided on request if they are not listed on the menu.
✉ Agios Christinias 4, Germasogeia village ☎ 05 325211 🕓 Closed Sun

Le Meridien (£££)
Three excellent restaurants serving French and international cuisine. Expensive but worth it.

✉ Old Limassol–Nicosia Road ☎ 05 634000 🕓 Daily

Mikri Maria (£)
Unusual and exceedingly small establishment in a backwater, run by two Cypriot women. Vegetarian dishes on request.
✉ 3 Angiras Street, Limassol ☎ 05 357679 🕓 Daily

Neon Phaliron (££)
Greek food, a great favourite with the locals for lunches and dinners.
✉ 135 Gladstone Street, Limassol ☎ 05 365768 🕓 Closed Wed, Sun evenings

Old Harbour (Ladas) (££)
Big fresh fish cooked on charcoal served in a fine traditional restaurant; very popular with locals. Some fish choices put it into a higher price category.
✉ Old Harbour, Limassol ☎ 05 365760 🕓 Daily

Pan Ku (££)
Chinese cuisine including Chow Mein and Chop Suey.
✉ Georgiou A, Potamos Germasogeia ☎ 05 322302 🕓 Daily

Yildizlar (££)
Fine Lebanese food.
✉ Old Limassol–Nicosia Road, near turning to Agios Tychon ☎ 05 322755 🕓 Closed Mon

Pissouri
Kastro (£)
Good food, friendly service.
✉ Pissouri beach 🕓 Daily

Zygi
Apovathra (££)
Good seafood in a fishing village.
✉ Seafront ☎ 04 332414 🕓 Daily

Carte Blanche
All attempts will be made to satisfy the faddiest of clients. The menu may include every wonderful item of Greek or Turkish cuisine, but if the customer wants egg and chips or something more obscure, the constituents will be procured, cooked and served with the same flourish as would befit the *à la carte* menu.

Pafos & the West

Hippo Kebabs
It is thought that when the first settlers came to Cyprus 11,000 years ago they found a ready supply of meat in the form of the pygmy hippopotamus. Although quite agile, it appears that the pig-sized animal was no match for hungry human hunters, who systematicaly drove it to extinction.

Coral Bay

Peyia Tavern (££)
Substantial meals of local dishes.
✉ Main Square, Pegeia
☎ 06 621077

Pafos

Argo (££)
Delicious moussaka and friendly service.
✉ Pafios Afrodites 21, Kato Pafos ☎ 06 233327 🕐 Daily

Avgerinos (££)
Individual restaurant with grilled fish dishes.
✉ Minous 4, Kato Pafos
☎ 06 232990 🕐 Daily

Chez Alex Fish Tavern (££)
Every kind of seafood from red mullet to kalamari. Lobster has to be ordered 12 hours in advance.
✉ Constantias 7, Kato Pafos
☎ 06 234767 🕐 Daily

Dover (££)
Extensive selection of hot and cold appetisers, followed by meat or fish courses; has a reputation for excellent seafood. Vegetarian menu available.
✉ Othellos Street, Aspasis Court, Kato Pafos ☎ 06 248100 🕐 Daily

Esperides Garden Restaurant (££)
Good quality local dishes at reasonable prices in a typical Pafos restaurant. The affable proprietor lived for many years in England.
✉ 28 Rodothea Court, Poseidonos Avenue, Kato Pafos ☎ 06 238932 🕐 Daily

Gondola (££)
Good Italian restaurant.
✉ Agios Antoniou 12, Kato Pafos ☎ 06 244717 🕐 Daily

Kavouri Taverna (££)
Above average local dishes.
✉ Artemidos Street, Kato Pafos ☎ 06 233376 🕐 Daily

Laona Restaurant (££)
Genuine traditional Cypriot dishes in pleasant atmosphere.
✉ Votsis Street 6, Pafos Old Town ☎ 06 237121 🕐 Daily, lunch only

Mother's Restaurant (££)
Wide selection of traditional Cypriot dishes and good basic meat meals. Special children's menu. The proprietor is a friendly sort and may well offer sightseeing advice to favoured diners.
✉ Basilica Centre, Apostolou Pavlou Avenue, Kato Pafos
☎ 06 236474 🕐 Daily

Taj Mahal (£££)
Exotic Indian dishes that are well presented.
✉ Tafon ton Vasileon Raod, Kato Pafos ☎ 06 238639
🕐 Daily

Trata Plaka (££)
Offers good swordfish and prawns.
✉ Poseidonos Avenue, Kato Pafos ☎ 06 516329 🕐 Daily

Polis

Chix Chox (££)
Local and international cuisine, served at relaxed Polis pace.
✉ Plateia Eroon, Polis
☎ 06 321669 🕐 Daily

Ttakas Bay Restaurant (££)
Good location on its own private beach and excellent food.
✉ Ttakas Bay on the coast below Neon Chorion village
☎ 06 321087

Nicosia & the High Troodos

Nicosia

Abu Faysal (££)
Pure Lebanese food enhanced by an attractive garden terrace and mansion-style interior.
 31 Klimentos Street
☎ 02 360353 🕓 Daily

Aegeon (£)
Strictly Greek food, tourists welcome but only in ones and twos. Book and record shop attached.
✉ 40 Ektoros Street ☎ 02 347522 🕓 Dinner only

Archontikou (££)
Typical local food with outdoor tables.
✉ Aristokiprou 27, Laiki Geitonia ☎ 02 450080 🕓 Daily

Bagatelle (£££)
This is a stylish restaurant for French cuisine at its best, in a nice setting.
✉ 16L Kyriakos Matsis Avenue ☎ 02 317870 🕓 Mon–Sat

Corona (££)
This simple restaurant has survived the test of time and continues to serve good traditional food, al fresco in summer.
✉ Orfeos 15, Agios Dometios ☎ 02 444223 🕓 Daily

Erenia (£)
Small establishment with excellent *meze*. Good, firendly atmosphere.
✉ 64a Archiepiskopou Kyprianou Avenue, Strovolos ☎ 02 422860 🕓 Daily

Grecos Tavern (£££)
Some unusual dishes and a marvellous vegetarian *meze*.
✉ 3 Menandros Street ☎ 02 474566 🕓 Mon–Sat, dinner only

Plaka Taverna (££)
Excellent *meze* in an extremely popular eating establishment. The outside tables in the square are always in demand.
✉ Archiepiskopou Makriou III Square ☎ 02 446498 🕓 Daily

Scorpios (£££)
Excellent *à la carte* French and Cypriot cuisine with first class service, a favourite of Nicosians. Cocktail bar upstairs.
✉ 3 Stassinou Street ☎ 02 445950 🕓 Daily

Trattoria Romantica (££)
Italian restaurant and steakhouse.
✉ 132 Evagoras Pallikaridi ☎ 02 377276 🕓 Daily

Kakopetria

Maryland at the Mill (££)
Splendid view and varied dishes. Trout is the house speciality. Popular with tourists.
✉ Kakopetria ☎ 02 922536 🕓 Daily

Platres

Kaledonia (££)
Basic but excellent food. *Meze* a speciality.
✉ Keldonia Building, Platres ☎ 05 421404 🕓 Daily

Mandra Gardens (££)
A village tavern offering the best local dishes, with Greek music and dancing.
✉ Near centre of Platres ☎ 05 421888 & 421601 🕓 Daily

Psilo Dendro (££)
The grilled trout is good, especially when washed down with a jug of local wine.
✉ Centre of Platres ☎ 05 421350 🕓 Daily

Nineteenth-century Fare
'The principal food of the Cypriotes consists of olives, beans, bread and onions.' wrote Sir Samuel Baker in *Cyprus as I Saw It* in 1879. These days a wider range of fare is available, although the olive remains ubiquitous.

The North

Skewer Cuisine
Kebab is a big favourite with the locals. On a summer evening in the suburbs the air is redolent with smouldering charcoal and slowly cooking meat on long skewers. The result is not normally less than delicious for the Cypriots are well practised in this culinary art.

Famagusta (Gazimağusa) Area

Agora (££)
Turkish Cypriot fare, speciality Kup Kebabi cooked in traditional earth ovens.
✉ **17 Elmas Tabya Sokagi, Famagusta** ☎ **3665364** 🕐 **Closed Sun**

Akdeniz (£)
Simple local dishes and friendly service.
✉ **Just north of Salamis Bay Hotel** ☎ **No tel** 🕐 **Daily**

Carli's (£)
Lively atmosphere, locally caught fish.
✉ **On the beach, Bogaz** ☎ **3712515** 🕐 **Daily**

La Cheminée (££)
French ambience and cuisine, attentive service.
✉ **17 Kemal Server Sokagi, opposite Palm Beach Hotel, Famagusta** ☎ **3664624** 🕐 **Closed Mon**

Cyprus House (££)
Turkish style food surrounded by classical relics and *objets d'art*; belly dancers give occasional performances.
✉ **Polat Pasa Bulvari, opposite telecommunications office, Famagusta** ☎ **3664845** 🕐 **Closed Sun**

Karsel (££)
Traditional fare in pleasant surroundings by the beach.
✉ **Mağusa Boğazi** ☎ **3712469** 🕐 **Daily**

Kemalin Yeri (££)
Fish is the mainstay but the kebab and *meze* is very edible.
✉ **Mağusa Boğazi** ☎ **3712515** 🕐 **Daily**

Kocareis (££)
Beach bar and restaurant, fresh seafood. Next to the Salamis Bay Hotel.
✉ **Salamis Yolu, Famagusta** ☎ **3788229** 🕐 **Daily**

Mini Bar Beach Restaurant (£)
The building may not be an architectural masterpiece, but the seafood is good.
✉ **Between Park Hotel and Salamis Bay Hotel, north of Famagusta** ☎ **No tel** 🕐 **Daily**

Onur (££)
Reasonably priced Turkish Cypriot food in friendly atmosphere. Music and dancing on Saturdays.
✉ **Opposite Giranel Hotel** ☎ **3765314** 🕐 **Daily**

Viyana (££)
Kebab dishes served in attractive shady garden.
✉ **Yesil Deniz Sokagi, Famagusta** 🕐 **Daily**

Kyrenia (Girne) and Surrounding Area

Alexandra's Restaurant (££)
Traditional dishes served in style, with panoramic views along the coast. The best chocolate mousse in town.
✉ **Karsiyaka village** ☎ **8252151** 🕐 **Closed Wed**

Ali Pasa (££)
Overlooking the sea. Very friendly reception. Free coffee.
✉ **Near Lapta** ☎ **8218942** 🕐 **Daily**

Allah Kerim (£)
Good atmosphere, lots of locals and free Turkish coffee.
✉ **Approx 13km west of Kyrenia to Alsancak** 🕐 **Daily**

Altinkaya (££)
Renowned for its fish dishes.
✉ Towards Lapta, 8km west of Kyrenia ☎ 8218341 ⏰ Daily

Birtat (£)
Good local cuisine. Free melon and coffee.
✉ Near Alsancak ⏰ Daily

Canli Balik (££)
Fresh fish and *meze* by the splendid harbour.
✉ Harbourside, Kyrenia ☎ 8152182 ⏰ Daily 9AM–2PM

The Crow's Nest (££)
British customers will feel at home with the good pub food and atmosphere in this high mountain village.
✉ Karaman village ☎ 8222567 ⏰ Daily

Duckworth House Restaurant (££)
Home cooking at reasonable prices. Swimming pool on hand for those who haven't eaten too much.
✉ Karaman village ☎ 8222513 ⏰ Daily

Efendi's (£)
Ottoman house in old quarter of Kyrenia. French cuisine using local ingredients. Booking advisable.
✉ Street behind harbour, near mosque ☎ 8151149 ⏰ Daily

Erols (£)
Local kebabs and *meze* cooked on a barbecue.
✉ Ozanköy village ☎ No tel ⏰ Daily

The Fisherman's Fez (£)
One can contemplate the restaurant's name while trying one of the varied traditional courses.
✉ Catalköy ☎ 8244600 ⏰ Daily

Grapevine (££)
International cuisine. Frequented by ex-pats at lunchtimes.
✉ Nicosia Road, Kyrenia ☎ 8152496 ⏰ 11AM–midnight. Closed Sun

Green Peace Restaurant (££)
Traditional Turkish dishes with very young guides watching, if needed, to take customers to Antiphonitis Monastery or nearby turtle beach.
✉ Esentepe village ☎ 8236350 ⏰ Daily

Halil's (££)
This is the place for authentic Turkish atmosphere. Halil and his staff are great extroverts. Excellent food
✉ West end of Kyrenia harbour, by Customs House ☎ No tel ⏰ Daily

Happy Garden Restaurant & Bar (£)
No-frills cuisine, speciality firin kebab and slow-cooked meat.
✉ Ozanköy village ☎ 8155715 ⏰ Daily

Harbour Club (£££)
Splendid view over harbour. Two restaurants, upstairs French cuisine and first-class seafood, downstairs typical Turkish dishes.
✉ Kyrenia Harbour (near castle) ☎ 8152211 ⏰ Closed Tuo lunch

Hideway (£)
Tasty dishes served in a very relaxing atmosphere, complete with a pool.
✉ West of Kyrenia on way to Karaman ☎ 8222620 ⏰ Daily

Isola Celesta (££)
International cuisine and some very interesting items.
✉ Karakum ☎ 8157770 & 8157771 ⏰ Daily

Jashan (££)
Indian cuisine and excellent service. Booking advisable.
✉ Edremit village ☎ 8222514 ⏰ Daily

Manners Maketh Man
'Do not start to eat before your elders. Always begin your meal by saying grace and eat with your right hand. Do not produce a knife at the table and do not strip a bone clean, do not be too voracious and do not slouch. Do not blow with your mouth over hot food. Eat in a measured manner, for a person should always eat and drink little.' Eleventh-century Turkish etiquette instructions.

The North

Always Room for One More

No Cypriot restaurateur has been known to turn custom away. The place may be packed, but somehow a space will be created, tables and chairs found with the tablecloth going on almost faster than the eye can see.

Kibele (£££)

The finest continental cuisine. The surroundings are very atmospheric.

✉ **Grounds of Bellapais Abbey, Beylerbeyi** ☎ **8157531** ⏱ **Daily, reservation advisable**

Kismet View (££)

Good simple local cuisine.

✉ **Oleander Road, Karaman** ☎ **8222594** ⏱ **Daily**

Lemon Tree (££)

An excellent fish restaurant, also good *meze*. Live music Fridays and Saturdays.

✉ **Catalköy Road, 5km east of Kyrenia** ☎ **8244045** ⏱ **Daily**

Levant Restaurant (££)

Very good near eastern food

✉ **Karman Village** ☎ **8222559** ⏱ **Daily**

Mirabelle Restaurant (££)

Good French cuisine.

✉ **1km outside Kyrenia on Karakum road** ☎ **8157390** ⏱ **7–10:30. Closed Mon**

Mountain House Restaurant (££)

Well-prepared international cuisine.

✉ **Bellapais Road, Kyrenia** ☎ **8153881** ⏱ **Daily**

Niazi's (££)

Excellent meat dishes, the cooking of kebabs has been turned into an art form.

✉ **West of the harbour, opposite Dome Hotel, Kyrenia** ☎ **8152160** ⏱ **5–11. Closed Wed**

Old Milos (£)

Traditional food in a lovely setting.

✉ **Alsancak** ☎ **8218939** ⏱ **Daily**

Olguns (£)

Turkish menu at more than reasonable prices.

✉ **Karaoğlanoğlu Village** ☎ **8222494** ⏱ **Daily**

Ottoman House (£)

Family-run restaurant specialising in home cooking.

✉ **Zeytinlik village, west of Kyrenia** ☎ **8153960** ⏱ **Daily**

Papillon (££)

Produces some splendid dishes.

✉ **Nicosia road, Kyrenia** ☎ **8152355** ⏱ **7–midnight Closed Mon**

Paradise (££)

Specialises in imaginative *mezes* and fish and kebab.

✉ **Catalköy Road, 5km east of Kyrenia** ☎ **8244397** ⏱ **Daily**

Rafters (££)

Bistro and pub in what is claimed to be the oldest olive grove in Cyprus. A full menu to suit all appetites. Booking advisable.

✉ **Ozanköy Road, 4km east of Kyrenia** ☎ **8152946** ⏱ **6–1, Sun from 11:30. Closed Thur**

Ramos (££)

Varied menu and good selection of wines.

✉ **1.5km east of Alsancak** ☎ **8218020** ⏱ **Daily**

Rita on the Rocks (£)

Very good fresh fish, booking advisable.

✉ **Just east of Lapta on main road to Kyrenia** ☎ **No tel** ⏱ **Daily**

Rose Gardens (££)

Varied food for all tastes.

✉ **Kilicaslan Sokagi, Lapta** ☎ **8218927** ⏱ **Daily**

Set Fish Restaurant (£)
Excellent seafood of all descriptions at low cost. By the harbour.

✉ **Harbourside, Kyrenia**
☎ **8152336** ⏰ **Daily**

Serket's (££)
Traditional dishes, fresh fish and vegetarian. Jacuzzi bathing for those not too replete.

✉ **Lapta, main road west of village** ☎ **8218077** ⏰ **Daily**

Tiberio (££)
European food in a stylish environment.

✉ **Just west of Kyrenia**
☎ **No tel** ⏰ **Daily**

Tree of Idleness (££)
Fish and kebab dishes and Turkish Cypriot *meze*.

✉ **Beylerbeyi** ☎ **8153380**
⏰ **Daily**

Yenihan Restaurant (££)
Very good Turkish fare.

✉ **20 Temmuz Caddesi, Kyrenia** ☎ **No tel** ⏰ **Daily**

Zlya's Bar Fish Restaurant (££)
Despite its good reputation for fish, the shish kebab and *meze* are also worth a try.

✉ **Catalköy village**
☎ **8244027** ⏰ **Daily**

North Nicosia

Annibal (££)
Traditional Turkish kebab house.

✉ **East end of Green Line by Famagusta Gate** ☎ **2274835**
⏰ **Daily**

Caglayan (££)
Popular restaurant.

✉ **Outside the walls off the Gazimağusa Road** ☎ **2278250**
⏰ **Daily**

Chinese House (££)
As the name suggests, traditional Chinese food.

✉ **Orient Hotel** ☎ **2277924**
⏰ **11:30–2, 7–late. Closed Sun**

Continental (££)
Excellent kebabs.

✉ **Ataturk Meydani, behind the Saray Hotel** ☎ **2275394**
⏰ **Daily**

Saray Hotel (££)
International and Turkish cuisine with an impressive view over the city. Comfortable surroundings and service.

✉ **Atatürk Meydani**
☎ **2273115** ⏰ **Daily**

Guzelyurt (Morfou) Area

Four Stars Restaurant and Night Club (££)
Varied local fare including *meze*, kebab and fish. Friendly service.

✉ **23 Dr Fazil Kuçük Bulvari**
☎ **7144705** ⏰ **Daily**

Kemal Buyukoglu Aile Restaurant (£)
Every kind of kebab features on the good-value menu.

✉ **Akçay** ☎ **7257769**
⏰ **Daily**

Liman Fish and Chips (£)
Uncomplicated menu, but no worse for that and the fish is claimed to be the freshest in Cyprus. Good value for a straightforward meal that won't break the bank.

✉ **Gemikonaği near Lefka**
☎ **7277579** ⏰ **Daily**

Mevsim Restaurant (£)
Kentucky fried chicken features among more traditional dishes.

✉ **Gemikonaği near Lefka**
☎ **7277596** ⏰ **Daily**

Government Price Controls
Anybody who feels there is an unusual similarity in menu prices displayed in a majority of restaurants and cafés is not mistaken. The reason is because the government exerts a measure of price control. Before the start of the season all restaurateurs must submit their menu prices to the authorities. Once approved they can be reduced but not increased. This interference with market forces is to reduce the opportunities for overcharging visitors. The government also fixes the prices of many items of food in the shops.

Larnaka &
the Southeast

Prices
Prices are per room per night, with breakfast, in high season

Republic of Cyprus
£ = up to C£40
££ = C£40 – C£80
£££ = above C£80

Northern Cyprus
£ = up to TL10,000,00
££ = TL10,000000–
     TL20,000000
£££ = above TL20,000000

No Room on the Island
In July 1992 Cyprus was said to be full. Leading holiday firms met with the Cyprus Tourism authorities to discuss fears that the island would burst at the seams during August. The crisis was brought about by an increase in tourists of 120 per cent.

Agía Napa

Dome Hotel (££)
A large four-star hotel overlooking two long sandy beaches. Lush gardens surround a good-sized swimming pool. Food and drink is reasonably priced.
✉ **Makronissos, Agía Napa**
☎ **03 721010**

Grecian Bay Hotel (£££)
Directly overlooking the bay, this top class hotel has an unrivalled range of facilities. Also has its own good beach.
✉ **Agía Napa** ☎ **03 721301**

Kermia Beach (£££)
Peaceful self-contained complex of studios and apartments with many facilities. The price is for an apartment for two. Although the buildings are modern, the location is terrific and the atmosphere restful.
✉ **4km east of Agía Napa**
☎ **03 721429**

Napa Sol (£)
Modest 35-bedroom hotel. A good-value option for Nissi Beach.
✉ **79 Nissi Avenue, Agía Napa**
☎ **03 722044**

Nissi Beach Hotel (££)
The first hotel to be built at this little bay, it stands right next to the beach.
✉ **Nissi Beach, Agía Napa**
☎ **03 721021**

Olympic Napa Hotel (£££)
A low-rise building in a quiet location to the west of the resort. The gardens are very pleasant and there is a children's playground.
✉ **Agía Napa** ☎ **03 722500**

Larnaka

Arion Hotel (£)
A 31-bedroom hotel in a town centre side street.
✉ **26 Galileo street**
☎ **04 650200**

Faros Village (££)
Bungalow hotel on clifftop near Cape Kition and its lighthouse.
✉ **Perivolia, 14km south of Larnaka** ☎ **04 422111**

Four Lanterns (Sunotel) (£)
Good town centre location, also on the seafront.
✉ **19 Athinon Avenue** ☎ **04 652011**

Lordos Beach Hotel (£££)
Good standard hotel, designed, built and run by the well-known Lordos Group.
✉ **Dhekalia Road**
☎ **04 647444**

Pavion Hotel (£)
For the budget traveller, right in the centre of town.
✉ **11 Faneromeni Street, Agios Lazaros Square** ☎ **04 656688**

Protaras

Anais Bay Hotel (£)
Small and somewhat intimate, set in gardens close to a beach (normally crowded).
✉ **Protaras** ☎ **03 831351**

Mimoza Hotel (££)
Relaxed atmosphere and located by a secluded sandy cove. Wide selection of shops, bars and restaurants.
✉ **5km from centre of Protaras**
☎ **03 832797**

Pernera Beach Hotel (££)
A medium sized hotel close to small beach.
✉ **Pernera** ☎ **03 831011**

Limassol &
the South

Rural Hideways

Agro tourism is the new buzz word for the Cypriot tourist authorities. The plan is to help proprietors renovate traditional houses in the villages to attract a different kind of tourist and spare the remainder of Cyprus the ravages of intensive development.

Limassol

Amathus Beach (£££)
Opulent and well situated including Roman tomb in garden.
✉ Amathous Avenue ☎ 05 321152

Atlantica Bay (££)
Medium sized hotel close to ancient Amathous. Completely refurbished in 1996. A useful feature is the underpass to the beach, cutting out the main road.
✉ Amathous Avenue ☎ 05 321023

Chez Nous Sunotel (£)
Medium-priced and well-run hotel, comfortably smaller than most, with pleasant pool in a leafy garden.
✉ Potamos Germasogeia ☎ 05 323033

Curium Palace (££)
An older style hotel located in town, and which has maintained high standards over the years. Antique furniture and friendly owner add to the armosphere. The Municipal Gardens with their small zoo are next door.
✉ 2 Byron Street ☎ 05 363121

Four Seasons (£££)
The hotel enjoys a good reputation, the interior design has been considered, and the swimming pool is quite

splendid. Thalassotherapy and seaweed treatments also on offer.
✉ Old Limassol–Nicosia Road, 9km east of town centre ☎ 05 310222

Le Meridien (£££)
Excellent in every respect including splendid indoor and outdoor pools. Sumptuous well-planned rooms and lawns that sweep down to the sea. High quality cuisine is offered in three restaurants with resident band and Cypriot folk evenings.
✉ Old Limassol–Nicosia road ☎ 05 634000

Miramare Beach Hotel (££)
The hotel was built before the great rush to develop Limassol's eastern coastline. It has become a favourite with British guests over the years. The nightlife of Potamos Germasogeia is close by.
✉ Potamos Germasogeia ☎ 05 321662

Le Village (£)
Cheap and friendly bed and breakfast place.
✉ 242 Leontios A Street ☎ 05 368126

Pissouri

Bunch of Grapes Inn (£)
A restored 100-year-old inn with 11 guest rooms, quite different to the usual modern hotel.
✉ Pissouri village ☎ 05 221275

Columbia Pissouri Beach (£££)
On its own, right on the fine sand beach; impressive Cape Aspro is to the west.
✉ Pissouri Beach ☎ 05 221201

Accommodation Guide
For the independent traveller the Cyprus Hotel Guide, free and published annually by the Tourism Organisation, is invaluable. Every hotel and guest house is listed, giving star rating, number of rooms and price.

Pafos & the West
Nicosia & the High Troodos

Picturesque Plumbing
The older Cypriot hotels are known for their erratic plumbing, quite apart from the fact that the drains cannot cope with toilet paper, taps being put on the wrong way round and showers which seem to have been adapted from water cannon are not uncommon.

Pafos

Agapinor (£)
Excellent small hotel, that's run by a friendly team.
✉ **26 Nikodemos Mylonas Street, Pafos Old Town**
☎ **06 233927**

Akamas Hotel (£)
Good value 18-room hotel.
✉ **14 Grivas Digenis Street, Polis** ☎ **06 322507**

Aloe (££)
Medium sized hotel, close to seafront.
✉ **Poseidon Avenue, Kato Pafos** ☎ **06 234000**

Annabelle (£££)
Renowned luxury hotel.
✉ **Poseidon Avenue, Kato Pafos** ☎ **06 238333**

Axiothea (£)
Small hotel between the old and new town.
✉ **2 Ivi Maliotis Street, Pafos**
☎ **06 232866**

Cynthiana Beach (££)
Spectacular location on rocky shore. Has a small private beach, fairly quiet.
✉ **Kissonerga, 8km north of Pafos** ☎ **06 233900**

Kings (£)
Small inexpensive hotel near the Tombs of the Kings.
✉ **Tombs of the Kings Road, Kato Pafos** ☎ **06 233497**

Marion (£)
Long established old style hotel.
✉ **Marion Street, Polis**
☎ **06 321216**

Paphos Beach (£££)
Enviable beach front location.
✉ **Poseidon Avenue, Kato Pafos** ☎ **06 233091**

Nicosia

Averof (£)
A very pleasant quiet traditional hotel with 25 rooms.
✉ **19 Averof Street, Nicosia**
☎ **02 463447**

Carlton (£)
Good value hotel in convenient central location.
✉ **13 Princess de Tyras Street**
☎ **02 442001**

Cleopatra (££)
A popular 75-room hotel, centrally located in the new town.
✉ **8 Florina Street** ☎ **02 445254**

Hilton Hotel (£££)
Nicosia's leading hotel, with a pool and a business centre. The Hilton Hotel was the rendezvous point chosen by the British Commander after the Turkish invasion of 1974, where all British citizens gathered to be taken in convoy to the British Sovereign bases and then out of the country to safety.
✉ **Archbishop Makarios Avenue** ☎ **02 377777**

Holiday Inn (£££)
Recently refurbished.
✉ **70 Regaena Street** ☎ **02 475131**

Edelweiss (£)
A small pleasant hotel.
✉ **Pano Platres** ☎ **05 421335**

Makris Sunotel (£)
Nicely situated hotel.
✉ **48 A Mamantos Street, Kakopetria** ☎ **02 922419**

Troodos Sunotel (££)
High and ideal location for exploring the Troodos.
✉ **Troodos** ☎ **05 421635**

The North

Famagusta

Altun Tabya (£)
Reasonably priced 14-room hotel inside the city walls. A restaurant opens for Turkish food in the evenings.
✉ 7 Kizilkule Yolu
☎ 3665363

Mimoza Hotel (££)
Right on the water's edge, along a sandy beach, near Salamis.
✉ Just north of Salamis
☎ 3788219

Salamis Bay Hotel (£££)
Impressive complex of 431 rooms close to the ruins of ancient Salamis. Plenty of facilities on offer.
✉ 11km northeast of Famagusta ☎ 3788200

North Nicosia

Konak Pansiyon (£)
Unpretentious good-value-for-money establishment.
✉ 21 Mevlevi Tekke Sokagi
☎ 2287167

Saray Hotel (££)
Excellent central location for shopping and sightseeing. Standards are high, making this a popular venue in Turkish Cypriot Nicosia. The balcony of the roof restaurant, serving traditional Cypriot and standard European fare, offers terrific views across Nicosia.
✉ Attaturk Medani
☎ 2283115

Kyrenia and the West

Bristol (£)
Central location and good value. Ideally placed for visitors not wishing to drive. Traditional restaurant, bar facilities and a garden.
✉ 42 Hurriyet Caddesi
☎ 8156570

British Hotel (£)
Good Kyrenia harbour location. Great views from the restaurant roof terrace.
✉ Kordonboyu, west end of harbour ☎ 815 2240

Dome Hotel (££)
Famous for its colonial past. The longest established hotel in Cyprus occupies a prime position on a rocky outcrop near the harbour. There is a sea water swimming pool and a casino.
✉ Kordonboyu Caddesi
☎ 8152453

Dorana Hotel (£)
Situated within easy walking distance of the shopping area and harbour. Despite the location amid the bustle of the centre, the Dorana is quite peaceful.
✉ West of the harbour
☎ 8153521

Soli Inn (£)
Seaside hotel near the ruins of Soli, in Guzelyurt Bay.
✉ Gemikonagi village
☎ 7277575

Mosquito Hunting
Visitors who are susceptible to mosquitoes should ensure that they patrol their rooms before retiring. Any idle insect reclining on the wall should be dispatched. Modern methods such as sprays are suitable for the squeamish, if they are not available then a suitably thick paperback book will prove an adequate substitute. A few nights rendered sleepless by the whine of the mosquito, are a powerful incentive to perfect the technique.

Monastic Retreats
Until quite recently the monasteries would always find a bed for a traveller. Today the monks are not as obliging, the nature of travelling has changed, and reservation is often required.

Souvenir, Handicraft & Leather Shops

Shopping Hours

May–Sept, Mon–Fri 8–1, 4–7, Sat 8–1; Oct–Apr, Mon–Fri 8–1, 2:30–5:30 Shops in tourist areas, north and south, will stay open later.

Breaking the Law

All Turkish made products are banned from the Greek part of Cyprus. Shopkeepers who break the law risk two years in prison or a fine of £1,400. In 1995 Body Shop apologised after Turkish made face flannels were found in one of its shops.

Larnaka and the Southeast

A Laïki Geitonia (traditional quarter) is slowly being refurbished in Larnaka at the south end of Zinonos Kiteios Street. 750m to the south on Bozkourt and Ak Deniz Streets are a number of pottery shops, including Photos and Fotinis and Stavros. Elenas workshop and Studio ceramics workshop can also be found in this area. Walking about and comparing prices first is a good idea.

The Cyprus Handicraft Service
✉ 6 Kisma Lysioti Street, Larnaka ☎ 04 630327

Kornos Village
Terracotta pottery is still produced here in the same way as 2,000 years ago.

Liopetri and Xylofagou Villages
Good solidly built baskets are made here.

Melpo Leather and Jewellery
A good selection of both.
✉ 16 Makarios Avenue, Agía Napa

New Famagusta Leather Shops
Wide range of leather goods sold.
✉ 2 Makariou, Agía Napa

Photis Tourist Handicraft Centre
A wide range of crafts.
✉ Ileos Pavlou Street, Larnaka

Stavrovouni – Agia Varnava Monastery
A talented monk paints icons to order.

Limassol and the South

A collection of traditional shops by the castle and another by the old harbour sell pottery and copper goods.

Aspelia Craft
This establishment specialises in high-quality works.
✉ Agora Shopping centre, junction of Anexartisias and Ágios Andreou Streets, Limassol

Costas Theodorou Ltd
Good quality leather goods at reasonable prices.
✉ 37 Athens Street ☎ 05 363964, also at 129 Anexartisias Street, ☎ 05 368031

Cyprus Handicraft Centre
Traditional Cypriot handicrafts made in Government-run workshops.
✉ 25 Themidos Street, Limassol ☎ 05 33018

Lefkara Village (➤ 49)
A wide range of silverware and lace products can be found on sale in the village. Purchasers should check that they are being offered the genuine article and not an import.

P and D Mayromatis
Discerning and varied selection of leather goods run by a Cypriot couple who lived for many years in England.
✉ 23 Koumanderis Street, Limassol ☎ 05 364710

Philips Shoe Factory
Every kind of boot and shoe you can think of including orthopaedic. Shoes can be specially made to order in two to three days.
✉ Zig Zag Street, Limassol ☎ 05 748893

Sam's Leatherware
Wide range of goods on sale with leather jackets a speciality.

✉ **1A Anexartisias Street**
☎ **05 362141, also at 21 Ifigenias Street** ☎ **05 345853**

Scaraveos Designs
The goods are not exactly arts and crafts but there are some modern and very unusual designs.

✉ **236 Ágios Andreou Street, Limassol** ☎ **05 360518**

Pafos and the West
Chryssorrogiatissa Monastery
The monks have built up a thriving icon painting business.

Cyprus Handicraft Service
Traditional Cypriot handicrafts made in Government-run workshops.

✉ **64 Apostolou Pavlou Avenue, Pafos** ☎ **05 362303**

Fyti Village
The villagers produce fine woven cloth, especially embroidered curtains.

Nicosia and the High Troodos
Cyprus Handicraft Centre
The centre was created after Turkish invasion to provide work for Greek Cypriots displaced from the north. A range of goods are for sale and there is a permanent exhibition of local crafts.

✉ **186 Athalassa Avenue, Nicosia** ☎ **0230524**

Another branch of the Cyprus Handicraft Centre is to be found in Laïki Geitonia in the walled city.

✉ **Konstantinou Palaiologou Avenue** ☎ **02 303065**

Foini Village
A reputation for pottery encourages many to make the long journey to this remote area.

Leventis Museum Gift Shop
Reproductions of historical artefacts including some interesting jewellery are on sale.

✉ **Ippokratous Street (Nicosia walled city)**

Moutoullas
Famed for its bottled drinking water, this mountain village also produces fine wooden basins and copper goods.

Omodos
The tourist trail now takes in Omodos and souvenir shops abound. The examples of traditional embroidery are well worth seeking out.

The North
Ceramic Centre
Largest pottery showroom in the north.

✉ **Ortakoy, 3km northwest of Nicosia** ☎ **2032302**

Dizayn 74
Pottery made on site while you watch.

✉ **Karaoglanoglu Village**
☎ **8152507**

Galerie Dundar
Local handicrafts and copperware.

✉ **15–17 Turkmen Sokagi, Kyrenia** ☎ **8152092**

Serdar Leather
Goods direct from the shop's factory.

✉ **31 Limon Yolu, Gazimagusa also at 5 Mecidiye Sokagi, Nicosia**

Silk Making
Cyprus has, until recently, a great tradition of silk making going back to the Byzantine period. The warm coastal climate and abundance of mulberry trees were ideal for the silkworms and the weaving of silk became a significant cottage industry. Production declined when rural areas turned to the cultivation of lemon groves instead.

Stores, Arcades, Markets & Jewellery Shops

Spectacles Savings
Cypriot opticians have spotted a gap in the market and offer special tourist services of a quick turn around for sight tests and spectacles, all provided at a fraction of the cost at home.

Stores & Arcades

Larnaka and the Southeast
Forum
The store is a relatively modest emporium, perhaps reflecting the lack of competition in Larnaka.
⊠ Ileos Pavlou Street, Larnaka

Woolworth and Super Department Store
A typical department store selling everything from records to jewellery. It also includes a food hall.
⊠ General Timagia Avenue
☎ 04 631111

Limassol and the South
Agora
An impressive modern arcade of 48 shops. Some quality clothes and footwear outlets and a first-rate craft shop.
⊠ Junction of Ágios Andreou and Anexartisias Streets, Limassol

Marios Shopping Centre
A good range of clothes, shoes, bags, accessories and gifts.
⊠ 88 Ágios Andreou Street, Limassol

Marks and Spencer
A visit is guaranteed to make the British visitor feel at home. Useful for forgotten T-shirts.
⊠ Makariou III Avenue, Limassol

Woolworth Olympia
The standard range of department store goods and an in-store food hall and bakery.
⊠ 28 Oktovriou Avenue
☎ 05 311133

Woolworth
Not quite the same as at home but not far.
⊠ Old Nicosia Road, Limassol (the coast road, 2km east of the zoo and gardens)

Zako
Famous through Cyprus, this store has not lost the art of selling haberdashery. Browse happily amongst buttons.
⊠ Koumandaria Street, Limassol

Pafos and the West
Titania Shopping Arcade
Shopping centres are new to Pafos. This one houses a collection of good shops.
⊠ West end of Poseidonos Avenue, Pafos

Woolworth
This is a very smart store which opened in 1996.
⊠ West end of Poseidonos Avenue, Pafos

Nicosia and the High Troodos
Capital Center
This was the first real shopping centre in Cyprus, and is still worth a look.
⊠ Makarios Avenue, Nicosia, just south of the junction with Evagoras Avenue

City Plaza
The basement is given over to food, and then there are three levels of upmarket shops, selling clothes, shoes and sportswear.
⊠ Makarios Avenue, Nicosia, 60m south of junction with Evagoras Avenue

Marks and Spencer
Modern fashions.
⊠ Makarios Avenue, Nicosia, 40m south of junction with Evagoras Avenue

Woolworth
It is very popular with the locals and comes complete with self-service restaurant.
✉ **Makarios Avenue, junction with Digeni Akrita** ☎ **02 447801**

The North
Evkaf Ishani Precinct
✉ **Girne Caddesi**

Galleria Arcade
Two storeys of relatively modern shops.
✉ **Arasta Sokagi**

Markets
Fruit sellers will usually be fairly imprecise about weighing goods, to the customer's advantage. It is common for a few extra plums to be added free of charge.

Larnaka and the Southeast
Municipal fruit and vegetable market.
✉ **Ermou Street, Larnaka**

Limassol and the South
Central Market
Fruit and vegetable market.
✉ **Saripolou Street, Limassol**

Municipal Market
A wide range of fruit and vegetables.
✉ **Genethliou Mitella Street, Limassol**

Pafos and the West
Municipal Market
Open air stalls selling fruit and vegetables.
✉ **Pafos old town, southern end of Fellahoglou Street**

Nicosia and the High Troodos
Municipal Market
✉ **Plateia Dimarchias, Nicosia walled city**

Open Air Market
A splendid place to buy fish, fruit and vegetables in the shadow of a mosque.
✉ **Constanza Bastion, Konstantious Avenue**

The North
Covered Bazaar
✉ **South side of Selimye Mosque, Nicosia**

Covered Bazaar
✉ **North end of Canbulat Yolu, Famagusta**

Okkes Dayi Market
✉ **Attaturk Caddesi, Kyrenia**

Jewellery Shops

Larnaka and the Southeast
Le Mioneaux
Copies of museum artefacts.
✉ **73 Zinonos Kiteios Street, Larnaka** ☎ **04 658106**

Santa Maria Jewellery
Gold jewellery on sale and repairs undertaken.
✉ **7 Makariou, Paralimni**

Limassol and the South
Bargilis Jewellery
Mainly precious stones.
✉ **72 Athens Street, Limassol** ☎ **05 354023**

Tonia Jewellery
Beautiful gold jewellery a speciality.
✉ **177 Ágios Andreou Street** ☎ **05 355244**

Pafos and the West
Athos Diamond Centre
Hand made jewellery.
✉ **Poseidonos Avenue, Lighthouse Court 79–80, Pafos** ☎ **06 234951**

Nicosia and the High Troodos
G Stephanides, Son and Co Ltd
Long-established family concern; excellent modern designs.
🌐 **23 Makarios Avenue** ☎ **02 444419**

Enthusiastic Sales Pitch
Cypriot shopkeepers will never admit defeat. If they cannot convince you that the size or colour is just right then your choice will be promised for tomorrow. The promise should not be taken too literally.

Fun Parks & Go-karting

The Lure of Water
The marinas and waterparks that have sprung up recently in Cyprus almost suggest that previously there was a lack of entertainment for children. Doubtless these expensive ventures will eventually pay off, but the sandy beaches, turquoise seas and swimming pools will always be the better attraction for children. On a cautionary note, as the sun shines fiercely throughout the summer, great care should be taken to avoid a holiday ruined by sunburn.

Larnaka and the Southeast
Agía Napa Luna Parks
There are Luna Parks (fun fairs) with rides and sometimes go-karting in all the major towns. Agía Napa has one adjacent to Waterworld and another about 800m southwest of the monastery.
⊠ **Agía Thekla Road and off Nissi Avenue** ⏱ **Daily; times vary, but are approx 9:30–8 (later at weekends)**

Larnaka Luna Parks
There are the usual fun-fair rides at Larnaka's two Luna parks.
⊠ **Municipal Gardens and on airport road** ⏱ **Daily; times vary, but approx 9:30–8 (later at weekends)**

Skycoasters Agía Napa
Amazing death-defying manoeuvres for sober, non-pregnant participants over 1m tall, with no health problems!
⊠ **Adjacent to Luna Park on Nissi Avenue** ⏱ **Apr–Oct, daily 10–8**

Waterworld Agía Napa
A variety of exciting water chutes includes Mount Olympus, Chariot Chase and the Serpentines, plus log rolling in the activity pool, river trips, spray columns and geysers, and much more. There are also cafés, an ice cream parlour and gift shop, and sculptures in terrific bad taste. Ideal for restless children bored with the beach, but not with water. A family afternoon out.
⊠ **5km from town along Agía Thekla Road** ☎ **09 523423/ 523424** ⏱ **Daily 10–7**

Limassol and the South
Limassol Luna Parks
There are the usual fun-fair rides at Limassol's two Luna parks. The long opening hours are useful for those coming off the beach.
⊠ **Adjacent to the Roussos Beach Hotel and Christaki Kranou Street, Potamos Germasogeia area** ⏱ **Daily; times vary, but approx 9:30–8 (later at weekends)**

Pafos and the West
Pafos Luna Parks
There are the usual fun-fair rides at the two Luna parks in Pafos.
⊠ **Apostolou Pavlou Avenue and Tourist Office Beach, east of seafront** ⏱ **Daily; times vary, but approx 9:30–8 (later at weekends)**

Nicosia and the High Troodos
Nicosia Luna Park
There are the usual fun-fair rides at this park, which is particularly popular for its go-karting facilities. Adults as well as children can burn off some energy.
⊠ **Vasileos Pavlou Street** ⏱ **Daily; times vary but are approx 9:30–8 (later at weekends)**

Tivoli Luna Park
This is a particularly good Luna park, with a variety of fun-fair rides, adjacent to the International State Fairground. Combine the two venues for an entertaining afternoon away from the beach or as a break from sightseeing.
⊠ **Elia Papakyriakou 10, Engkumi** ☎ **02 352245/351231/ 351236** ⏱ **Daily; times vary, but approx 9:30–8 (later at weekends)**

Zoos, Rides & Other Activities

Larnaka and the Southeast

Agía Napa Marine Park
Four dolphins put on displays for spectators; two seals complete the line-up. Have a photograph taken with them or, by prior arrangement, swim with them. The complex also has a miniature railway.

✉ **Beach Road, between Nissi Beach and Sunwing Hotel** ☎ **03 723733** 🕐 **Mid-Feb–Oct**

Glass-bottomed Boats
See the Mediterranean's aquatic life in its natural habitat in comfort.

✉ **Agía Napa Harbour** ☎ **09 535636** 🕐 **Daily in summer**

Pony Riding
Rides on ponies for children are available in the Troodos Mountains.

✉ **Troodos Square** 🕐 **Most summer days**

Limassol and the South

Limassol Reptile House
Native lizards and more exotic creatures, including crocodiles.

✉ **Old Harbour**

Limassol Zoo
Various animals, including an elephant, kept in rather cramped conditions. There is also an aviary.

✉ **Municipal Gardens, 28 Aktovriou Street** 🕐 **Daily 9–1, 2:30–6:30**

Pafos and the West

Camel Riding
There is occasionally a camel offering rides in Pafos on the open land at the back of the harbour.

✉ **Behind the harbour** 🕐 **Summer; times vary**

Glass-bottomed Boats
See the aquatic life of Pafos Harbour.

✉ **Pafos Harbour** ☎ **09 535636** 🕐 **Daily in summer**

Kites
The Pafos Municipality organises a kite-flying competition in the Byzantine Castle area near the harbour. It takes place in the first or second week in March and is open to all comers. The colourful event is followed by a traditional feast.

✉ **Kyriakou Nikolaou Street** ☎ **06 232014**

Pafos Aquarium
An array of colourful fish from the oceans, seas and rivers of the world. The various fish tanks are built into a series of illuminated caves.

✉ **Off Poseidonos Avenue, near Theokepasti Church, Kato Pafos** ☎ **06 253920** 🕐 **Daily 10–8**

Snake George's Reptile Park
Cyprus reptiles and amphibians in their specific habitats.

✉ **15km north of Pafos on coastal road to Ágios Georgios, behind BP petrol station** ☎ **06 238160** 🕐 **Daily 9–sunset**

Nicosia and the High Troodos

Ostrich Farm Park
See the fastest two-legged creatures on earth at what claims to be Europe's largest ostrich farm. Visitors can have their photograph taken on an ostrich egg, and there is an exhibition centre, playground and barbecue area.

✉ **Ágios Giannis Malountas** ☎ **02 366178/465321 (Nicosia office)** 🕐 **Wed 3–8, Sat, Sun 10–8**

Admission Prices
Entry into the Luna parks is free. However, the more innovative and exciting rides/experiences are expensive. Water parks with their impressive features are also expensive. The skycoaster is particularly pricey.

Theatre & Cultural Events

Doubtful Directions
Some of the activities listed on these pages entail trips into the quieter parts of Cyprus. The visitor, if lost or doubtful of the route, should beware of directions given by villagers. They will be anxious to please and in an attempt not to disappoint may assume an unjustifiable knowledge with likely severe inconvenience for the gullible enquirer.

Easter is still the busiest time of year in Cyprus's festival calendar. The pre-Lenten Carnival starts proceedings with 10 days of entertainments and feasting, finishing on Green Monday, an occasion for family picnics in the country. Extravagantly decorated floats parade through Limassol. Green Monday is 50 days before Easter Sunday, and Holy Week begins on Palm Sunday, the Sunday before Easter. Religious icons all over the island get shrouded in black on Maundy Thursday. On Good Friday a solemn mass takes place, followed by a procession in which Christ's image is paraded through the streets. The shrouds are lifted from the icons on Easter Saturday, there are more processions and bonfires and fireworks are lit. Feasting takes place on Easter Sunday.

Larnaka and the Southeast
Agía Napa Festival (September)
In front of monastery with folk music and dancing.

Larnaka Festival (July)
Dance, theatre and music at the fort and the Municipal Amphitheatre, Artemedos Avenue.
☎ Further information 04 657745

Limassol and the South
Ancient Greek Drama Festival (June–August)
Performances of Classical drama are held in the amphitheatre at Kourion and other open-air theatres in the area.

Limassol Festival
Limassol Municipality organises theatre, music and dance events throughout the summer.
☎ Further information on 05 363103

Wine festival
A very popular event during the first week in September. Music, dance and wine tasting in the Municipal Gardens.

Nicosia and the High Troodos
British Council
Various cultural events in English.
✉ Museum Street ☎ 02 444840

Goethe Institute
German cultural events.
✉ 21 Markos Drakos Avenue ☎ 02 462608

Municipal Theatre
Regular performances by local and international companies.
✉ Museum Street ☎ 02 463028

Pafos and the West
Pafos Festival
Pafos Municipality organises theatre, music and dance events throughout the summer at the Odeion amphitheatre and the harbour fort.
☎ Further information 06 232804

The North
A variety of seminars and other cultural events take place throughout the year. Contact the centre in Northern Nicosia for details.
✉ Attatürk Cultural Centre Northern Nicosia

Sporting Activities

Angling

Fishing is permitted in 16 dams around the island subject to the purchase of a licence. Licences can be bought from the local Fisheries Department offices. Sea fishing is also possible from all the main coastal resorts.

Specialist angling holidays are also available from the UK. For details, contact:
Cyprus Angling Holidays
☎ 01732 450749

Larnarka and the Southeast
Achna Dam
Licences from Larnaka Fisheries Department.
✉ Piale Pashia Avenue
☎ 04 630294

Limassol and the South
Dipotamos Dam – east of Lefkara
Germasogeia Dam
Kourris Dam
Kalavassos Dam
Lefkara Dam
Licences from Fisheries Department
✉ Limassol Harbour ☎ 05 330470

Nicosia and the High Troodos
Kafizes Dam
Kalopanagiotis Dam
Lefka Dam
Lympia Dam
Palaichori Dam
Xyliatos Dam

Pafos and the West
Asprokremmos Dam
Mavrokalymbos Dam
Evretou Dam
Licences from Fisheries Department.
✉ Pafos Harbour ☎ 06 240268

Bird Watching

Cyprus is on the main migration routes for birds coming from Europe to Africa. There are about 98 species resident on the island and 200 more are regular visitors including 10,000 flamingos who winter on the Salt Lakes. More information is available from:
Cyprus Ornithological Society
✉ 4 Kanaris Street, Nicosia
☎ 02 420703

Bowling (ten pin)

General information from Cyprus Bowling Association
✉ PO Box 5287 ☎ 02 350085

Limassol and the South
Limassol Bowling
✉ Argyrokastrou Street, Limassol ☎ 05 370414
🕐 2pm–midnight

Nicosia and the High Troodos
Kykko Bowling
✉ behind Ledra Hotel, Nicosia
☎ 02 350085 🕐 1pm–2am

Cycling

Bikes can be hired in most resorts and there are also mountain-biking opportunities. The island's terrain is perfect for this. Sunglasses and hat are advisable in summer.

Cyprus Cycling Federation
✉ PO Box 4572, Nicosia ☎ 02 456344

Cyprus Mountain Bike Association
☎ 02 356174
Mountain-biking holidays – contact Argo Holidays London.
☎ 0171 331700

Shooting

Hunting, mainly the shooting of migratory birds, is a common pursuit in the rural areas, much to the despair of environmental groups. Attempts to ban or restrict the annual slaughter have failed to date.

111

Sporting Activities

Locals and Swimming
For a long time the local population seemed somewhat baffled by the visiting tourist's passion for the beach. They are coming to terms with the phenomenon, although even now, for most of the year, Cypriots feel that the sea is far too cold to comtemplate swimming.

Cyprus Car Rally
This takes place every year on the last weekend in September and is part of the European Championship. It is one of the toughest courses in the championship with winding dirt tracks and mountain roads.
For information contact:
Cyprus Automobile Association
✉ **PO Box 2279, Nicosia**
☎ **02 313233**

Diving
There are diving centres and sub-aqua clubs in all the seaside towns and at a number of the larger hotels. Cyprus is surrounded by clear waters, with coral, sponges, sea anemones, shells and colourful fish, giving great views to divers.

Football
There is a local league with 90 teams in four divisions and there are football pitches in all the main towns. There are also four teams which compete on an international basis.
KOP (Cyprus Football Federation)
☎ **02 445341**

Limassol and the South
Tsirio Stadium
Limassol
International football matches

Golf
This is a relatively new sport to Cyprus but there are now three golf courses on the island.

Pafos and the West
Tsada (18 hole course)
Set in the grounds of a 12th-century monastery, in a valley. Facilities include a restaurant, tennis and outdoor pool.
✉ **North of Pafos** ☎ **06 642774**

Secret Valley (18 hole course)
Set in a scenic valley surrounded by rock formations. Good facilities.
✉ **East of Pafos near, Petra Tou Romiou** ☎ **06 642774**

Pareklissa (9 hole course)
✉ **Elias Beach Hotel, east of Limassol** ☎ **05 325000**

Hang Gliding
This takes place in the Kyrenian Mountains and is promoted by the North Cyprus Turkish Aviation Association, based at Nicosia Airport.

Horse-racing

Nicosia and the High Troodos
Meetings are held at weekends throughout the year; on Sunday afternoon from January to mid-May and September to December, and on Saturday afternoon from mid-May to the end of July.

Nicosia Race Course
✉ **St Paul's Street, west of the city centre** ☎ **02 497966**

Horse Riding

Limassol and the South
Elias Beach Horse Riding Centre.
Lessons are available, with headgear provided. Trekking can be enjoyed in nearby countryside.
✉ **8km east of Limassol**
☎ **05 325000**

Nicosia and the High Troodos
Lapatsa Sports Centre
Headgear and footwear is sold at the centre's shop. An average number of horses and ponies. Tuition in dressage, show-jumping and cross country.

✉ **Near Pano Deftera** ☎ **02 621201**

Horses and ponies can be hired for trekking through the Troodos hills, usually starting from Troodos Square.

Pafos and the West
Pafos Riding Centre
✉ **Near Tombs of The Kings**

Sailing

Larnaka and the Southeast
Larnaka Nautical Club
☎ **04 623399**

Larnaka Marina has facilities for visiting yachts.
☎ **04 653110**

Limassol and the South
Limassol Nautical club
☎ **05 324282**

St Raphael Harbour
✉ **Limassol**
☎ **05 321100**

Pafos and the West
Pafos Nautical Club
☎ **06 233745**

The North
Yachts may be moored in Kyrenia harbour.
Dolphin Sailing
Dinghies, para sailing, speed boat and aqua rocket trips Denis Kizi beach, May–Oct.

Shooting
General information on all the clubs is available from:
Cyprus Shooting Association
✉ **PO Box 3931, Nicosia**
☎ **02 367043**

Larnaka and the Southeast
Famagusta District Shooting Club
The club is located behind the old Roman aqueduct.
✉ **Just outside Paralimni on road to Sotira** ☎ **03 827000**
🕐 **Mon–Sat**

Larnaka Shooting Club
✉ **4km northwest of the city centre at Kamares** ☎ **04 654378** 🕐 **Wed & Sat**

Limassol and the South
Limassol Shooting Club
✉ **Near Polimidia, 8km northwest of city centre on Troodos road** ☎ **05 355572**
🕐 **Tue–Sun**

Nicosia and the High Troodos
Nicosia Shooting Club
✉ **8km southeast of the city centre** ☎ **02 482660**
🕐 **Tue–Sun**

Pafos and the West
Pafos Shooting Club
✉ **12km east of Pafos on old Limassol Road** ☎ **06 232109**
🕐 **Wed & Sat**

Skiing

Nicosia and the High Troodos
Mount Olympus
The season runs from January until March
Four runs of about 200m in Sun Valley.
Five more longer, more demanding runs on the north face.
Two tracks for cross country skiers.
Ski equipment can be hired in Sun Valley.
Mount Olympus is situated 3km from the Troodos hill resort and around an hour's drive from both Limassol and Nicosia.
The Ski Club
✉ **PO Box 2185 Nicosia**
☎ **02 365340**

Skiiers Dilemma
Skiing enthusiasts have a dilemma. At weekends they need to get to the ski shop early before the best gear is given out, but if there has been overnight snow they will be lucky to get their cars up the last section of Mount Olympus if they beat the snow plough. Another reason for getting on the slopes early is that the snow soon turns to mush in the mid-morning heat, powder snow is a rarity.

Sporting Activities & Walking

Water Skiing
Discounts can be negotiated for the promise to turn up every day. However, almost certainly the boat will be broken down, or elsewhere when it is wanted. In addition an eye should be kept on the time allocation, for mysterious laws of relativity tend to make the driver's watch run faster than the skiers.

Swimming
The extensive coastline offers excellent opportunities for swimmers. Red buoys indicate swimming areas. Most beaches offer safe bathing, but there are some beaches in the Pafos area which can be dangerous in rough weather and warning notices should be heeded. The beach at Kourion is also unsafe.

Larnaka and the Southeast
Larnaka public beach
Changing facilities and café on site. Free entry.
✉ 10km east of Larnaka
☎ 04 644511

Limassol and the South
Dhassoudi public beach
Changing facilities and café on site. Free entry.
✉ 5km east of Limassol
☎ 05 322811

Pafos and the West
Geroskipou
Changing facilities and café on site. Free entry.
✉ 3km east of Pafos
☎ 06 234525

Swimming Pools

Nicosia and the High Troodos
Nicosia Olympic Pool
West side of the town.

Limassol and the South
Limassol Pool
Next to Dhassoudi beach.

Larnaka and the Southeast
Larnaka Pool
Municipal Sports centre in the middle of the town.

Pafos and the West
Pafos Pool
Northeast of the old town, Agiou Dionysiou Street

Watersports
Swimming, diving and sailing, windsurfing and water skiing are possible at all the resorts, south and north.

Tennis
There are tennis courts in most of the larger hotels and municipal courts in the main towns.

Walking
Midsummer is much too hot for this pastime; even the mountain temperatures prove too high for most people. As a result, many visitors to Cyprus are enthusiastically turning to walking in the cooler months. The Cypriot, however, remains to be converted; the idea that anyone would wish to travel more than a short distance on foot for pleasure is incomprehensible to many.

Consequently, until recently at least, there were no ramblers' paths or trails. Any routes discovered had a strictly utilitarian purpose related to farming or hunting and rarely went where the rambler wished to go.

There are numerous opportunities for walking in the mountains. Large scale maps will be needed on most occasions. The British Ministry of Defence series is invaluable. Try the Department of Lands and Survey in Nicosia for copies (☎ 02 403390).

In the north walkers will have problems with access as many of the mountain areas are closed off due to the presence of the military.

All walkers should remember that even at high altitude the weather can be very hot and that anyone undertaking a strenuous walk or climb should take water with them. Conversely, those walking in winter should realise that many of the mountains are very high and that bad weather is common and they should dress accordingly.

Nicosia and the High Troodos

There are four walking trails in the Troodos Region. These have been designed by the Cyprus Tourism Organisation (CTO) which provides helpful leaflets listing all the flora, geology and other natural items of interest.

The trails themselves are not always that well marked on the ground, and the tourist office leaflet is not as detailed as it could be, so walkers will need to keep their wits about them and use their own initiative at times.

Forest roads abound. They are gouged out of the hillside regularly by the Forestry Department and are everywhere in the Troodos Mountains. For walkers they are really something of a last resort as they generally follow every twist and turn of the contour line they happen to be on, resulting in about two miles travelled for every genuine mile gained.

Artemis Trail
The trail is named after Artemis (Diana), the ancient goddess of forests.

A high level circuit of 6.5km around Mount Olympus starting a short distance up the main road to the summit.

Atalante Trail
The trail is named after the mythological forest nymph. Starts from Troodos Post Office and is 9km long.

After about 3km from the start point the trail reaches a spring of clean drinking water. There are wooden benches at various points along the way.

Kaledonia Trail
This is also known as 'the trail of nightingales' due to its warbling birds. The start is reached by turning off the Platres Road heading down to the summer Presidential residence.

The trail runs along the banks of the river to the falls and is 3km long. In summer this cool ravine is refreshing, and thick shade is provided by trees.

Persephone Trail
This trail is named after the goddess of spring. It offers beautiful scenery. It starts just south of Troodos Square and is about 6.5km there and back.

Pafos and the West
Akamas Trails
In the Akamas there are two trails. Both start from the Baths of Aphrodite and are both about 7.5km long, initially heading west of the Baths before going their separate ways.

Countryside Care
You are kindly requested not to litter the countryside, cut flowers or plants, or damage structures. Such actions contravene the Forest Law and offenders face prosecution.

What's On When

Traditional Festivals

The Greek Cypriots have a wealth of traditional festivals and fairs. Many derive from the Greek Orthodox Church, others have pagan origins. Despite this rich heritage the number of events grow. There are now beauty contests, Olympic Day 10-km runs, beer festivals, dog shows and annual exhibitions of coinage.

January

New Year's Day (1 Jan)
Epiphany (6 Jan): one of the most important Greek Orthodox religious celebrations of the year

March

Greek National Day (25 Mar): parades and celebrations

April

National Day (1 Apr): anniversary of the EOKA uprising
Turkish Children's Festival (23 Apr)

May

Labour Day (1 May)
May Fair in Pafos (1 May): 10 days of cultural events and exhibitions of Cypriot flora, basketwork and embroidery
Anthestiria Flower Festivals (early May): the festivals' origins go back to celebrations honouring the god Dionysos in Ancient Greece
Turkish Youth Festival (19 May)
Cyprus International Fair (late May): the largest trade fair in Cyprus, held in Nicosia and lasting 10 days

July

Larnaka Festival (throughout Jul): performances of dance and theatre in the fort and the Pattichon amphitheatre

August/September

Turkish Communal Resistance Day (1 Aug)
Turkish Victory Day (30 Aug)
Limassol Wine Festival (late Aug–first week in Sep): a 12-day indulgence of free wine, with music and dance some evenings

October

Independence Day (1 Oct)
Greek National Day (28 Oct): also known as Ochi Day.

Student parades all over southern Cyprus
Turkish National Day (29 Oct)

November

Proclamation of Turkish Republic of North Cyprus (15 Nov)

December

Christmas Day (25 Dec)

Moveable Feasts

Apokreo Festivities (50 days before Orthodox Easter): two weeks of fun in most towns. Limassol has fancy dress balls and children's parades.
Green Monday (50 days before Orthodox Easter): a day of laughter, funny disguises and vegetarian picnics in the country.
Procession of Ágios Lazaros Icon, Larnaca (eight days before Orthodox Easter Sun): a special mass service in memory of Ágios Lazaros followed by an impressive procession carrying his icon through the town.
Easter: the biggest Greek Orthodox religious feast. On the Sunday, celebrations last all day.
Kataklysmos, Festival of the Flood (50 days after Easter, coinciding with Pentecost): celebrations take place in all the seaside towns and include dancing, folk singing, swimming competitions and boat races
Agía Napa Festival (late Sep): a weekend of folk music, dance and theatre, combined with agricultural exhibitions
Seker or Ramazan Bayram: a three-day feast at the end of the Ramadan fast.
Kurban Bayram: four days during which lambs are traditionally sacrificed and shared with the needy.

Practical Matters

TIME DIFFERENCES

GMT
12 noon

Cyprus
2PM

Germany
1PM

USA (NY)
7AM

Netherlands
1PM

Spain
1PM

BEFORE YOU GO

WHAT YOU NEED

● Required
○ Suggested
▲ Not required

	UK	Germany	USA	Netherlands	Spain
Passport/National Identity Card	●	●	●	●	●
Visa (➤ 119, Arriving)	▲	▲	▲	▲	▲
Onward or Return Ticket, Republic of Cyprus	●	●	●	●	●
Onward or Return Ticket, Northern Cyprus	▲	▲	▲	▲	▲
Health Inoculations	▲	▲	▲	▲	▲
Travel and Health Insurance (➤ 123, Health)	○	○	○	○	○
Driving Licence (national with English translation or International)	●	●	●	●	●
Car Insurance Certificate (if own car)	●	●	●	●	●
Car Registration Document (if own car)	●	●	●	●	●

WHEN TO GO

Coastal Cyprus

████████ High season

▭ Low season

17°C	17°C	19°C	23°C	26°C	30°C	32°C	33°C	31°C	27°C	22°C	19°C
JAN	FEB	MAR	APR	MAY	JUN	JUL	AUG	SEP	OCT	NOV	DEC

🌧️ Very wet   🌧️ Wet   ☁️ Cloud   ☀️ Sun

TOURIST OFFICES

In the UK
Cyprus Tourist Office
213 Regent Street
London W1R 8DA
☎ 0171 734 9822
Fax: 0171 287 6534

Northern Region of
Cyprus Tourist
Information Office
29 Bedford Square
London WC1B 3EG
☎ 0171 631 1930
Fax: 0171 631 1873

In the USA
Cyprus Tourism
Organisation
13 East 40th Street
New York
NY 10016
☎ 212/683 5280
Fax: 212/683 5282

Northern Region of
Cyprus Tourist
Information Office
1667 K Street, Suite
690, Washington
DC 20006
☎ 202/887 6198
Fax: 202/467 0685

POLICE 112 (Republic)	**155 (North)**
FIRE 112 (Republic)	**199 (North)**
AMBULANCE 112 (Republic)	**112 (North)**
FOREST FIRES 1407 (Republic)	

WHEN YOU ARE THERE

ARRIVING

The national airline, Cyprus Airways (☎ 02-443054) operates scheduled flights from Britain and mainland Europe to Larnaka and Pafos. There are no direct flights to North Cyprus, you fly via Turkey for which you need a visa if you intend visiting.

Larnaka Airport
Kilometres to city centre

5 kilometres

Journey times	
🚆	N/A
🚌	30 minutes
🚍	20 minutes

Ercan Airport
Kilometres to Nicosia

23 kilometres

Journey times	
🚆	N/A
🚌	35 minutes
🚍	15 minutes

MONEY

The currency of the Republic of Cyprus is the Cyprus pound (C£), divided into 100 cents. Coins are in denominations of 1, 2, 5, 10, 20 and 50 cents; notes C£1, 5, 10 and 20.

The currency of North Cyprus is the Turkish lira (TL). Coins are TL100, 500, 1,000, 2,500, 5,000, 10,000, 25,000 and 50,000; notes TL10,000, 20,000, 50,000, 100,000, 250,000, 500,000, 1,000,000 and 5,000,000.

TIME

 Cyprus is two hours ahead of Greenwich Mean Time (GMT+2), but from late March, when clocks are put forward one hour, to late October, summer time (GMT+3) operates.

CUSTOMS

 YES

Goods Obtained Duty Free taken into Republic of Cyprus (Limits):
Alcohol (over 22° vol): 1L *and* Wine: 0.75L
Cigarettes: 200 *or*
Cigarillos: 100 *or*
Cigars: 50 *or*
Tobacco: 250gms
Perfume and Toilet Water: 300ml (not more than 150ml of perfume)
Goods Obtained Duty Free taken into North Cyprus (Limits):
Alcohol (over 22° vol): 1.5L *and* Wine 1.5L
Cigarettes: 400 *or*
Cigarillos: 200 *or*
Cigars: 100 *or*
Tobacco: 500gms
Perfume: 100ml
Toilet Water: 100ml
You must be 18 and over to benefit from the alcohol and tobacco allowances.

 NO
Drugs, firearms, ammunition, offensive weapons, obscene material, unlicensed animals, fruit, nuts, vegetables, cut flowers, bulbs and seeds.

EMBASSIES/HIGH COMMISSIONS/CONSULATES

Republic of Cyprus (none in North Cyprus)

UK (British High Commission) (02) 473131/7	Germany (Embassy) (02) 444362/3/4	USA (Embassy) (02) 476100	Netherlands (Consulate) (05) 366230	Spain (Consulate) (02) 433151

WHEN YOU ARE THERE

TOURIST OFFICES

Republic of Cyprus

- Cyprus Tourism Organisation
  Léoforos Lemesou 19
  PO Box 4535
  CY 1390 Nicosia
  ☎ (02) 337715
  Fax: (02) 331644

- Aristokyprou 35
  Laïki Geitonia
  CY 1011 Nicosia
  ☎ (02) 444264

- Spyrou Araouzou 15
  CY 3036 Limassol
  ☎ (05) 362756

- Georgiou A' 35
  CY 4040 Germasogeia
  ☎ (05) 323211

- Plateia Vasileos Pavlou
  CY 6023 Larnaka
  ☎ (04) 654322

- Gladstonos 3
  CY 8046 Pafos
  ☎ (06) 232841

- Léoforos Kryou Nerou 12
  CY 5330 Agía Napa
  ☎ (03) 721796

- CY 4820 Platres
  ☎ (05) 421316

North Cyprus

- Nicosia
  ☎ 2289112 or 2289629

- Kyrenia
  ☎ 8152145

- Famagusta
  ☎ 3662864

OPENING HOURS REPUBLIC

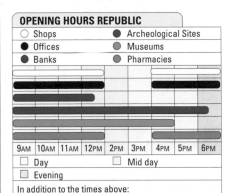

In addition to the times above:
Republic of Cyprus Offices, shops and pharmacies close Wednesday and Saturday PM. Afternoon hours are 2:30 to 5:30 (offices 3 to 6) October to April. Banks open 8:15 July, August, Monday 3:15 to 4:45 all year. Banks in main tourist areas open afternoons. Most museums close for lunch and also one day a week.

OPENING HOURS NORTH

○ Shops	● Archeological Sites
● Offices	● Museums
● Banks	● Pharmacies

9AM	10AM	11AM	12PM	2PM	3PM	4PM	5PM	6PM

□ Day	□ Mid day
□ Evening	

In addition to the times above:
North Cyprus Shops and pharmacies open 8 to 1 and 2 to 6 in winter and shut Saturday PM in summer. In winter offices open 8 to 1 and 2 to 5; banks open 8 to 1 and 2 to 5; museums open 8 to 1 and 2:30 to 5.

**DRIVE ON THE
LEFT**

**TOILETS
CHARGE**

PUBLIC TRANSPORT

Cross-Island Buses Republic of Cyprus: Intercity and village buses operate frequently between towns and various holiday resorts with many trips per day. Almost all villages are connected by local buses to nearest towns but services operate only on weekdays once a day leaving early in the morning, returning to the villages in the afternoon. North Cyprus: Except for the main routes such as Nicosia to Kyrenia, buses are infrequent and do not run to a timetable and your fellow passengers are more likely to be soldiers than tourists.

Boat Trips Republic of Cyprus: One-day boat excursions (including lunch) operate from May to October. Popular trips include: Limassol Harbour to Lady's Mile Beach; Pafos Harbour to Coral Bay and Pegeia; Agía Napa to Paralimni and Protaras coast; Larnaka Marina along Larnaka, Agía Napa and Protaras coast; and Latsi along the Akamas coast. North Cyprus: From May to October there are boat trips (including lunch) from Kyrenia Harbour to the beaches at Acapulco or Mare Monte (☎ 8153708).

Urban Transport Republic of Cyprus: Urban and suburban buses operate frequently only during the day (starting very early in the morning) between 5:30AM and 7PM. During summer, in certain tourist areas, buses may operate until midnight. It is a good idea to check routes with your hotel.
North Cyprus: There is a good bus service within the main towns, with buses running approximately every half hour. Check with your hotel for more detailed information.

CAR RENTAL

Many firms, including the internationally known, though mainly local ones in the north. Cars are expensive in the Republic, cheap in the north. Cars in both sectors bear distinctive red number plates starting with a 'Z' and sometimes are in poor condition.

TAXIS

In the Republic service taxis (*dolmus*), shared with other people (4 to 7 seats) operate between main towns every half hour. There are also rural taxis which operate in hill resorts and urban taxis in towns. In the north taxis can only be found at taxi stands.

DRIVING

Speed limits on motorways and dual carriageways: **110kph; min 65kph (north Cyprus: 60mph)**

Speed limits on country roads: **80kph (north Cyprus: 40mph)**

Speed limits on urban roads: **50kph, or as signposted (north Cyprus: 30mph)**

Must be worn in front seats at all times and in rear seats where fitted.

Random breath-testing. Limit: 39 micrograms of alcohol (59 north) in 100ml of breath.

Petrol in the Republic of Cyprus costs as much as any in Europe. In the north it is cheaper. Grades sold in the south are super, regular, unleaded and diesel. In the north unleaded petrol is not sold. Petrol stations in the south are open 6AM to 6PM; closing 4PM Saturdays, many on Sundays. In the north they may open until 9 or 10PM.

If you break down in the Republic of Cyprus 24-hour towing facilities are provided by the Cyprus Automobile Association in Nicosia (☎ 02-313131), which is affiliated to the Alliance International de Tourisme (AIT).
If the car is hired follow the instructions given in the documentation.

PERSONAL SAFETY

The police are relaxed and helpful and English is widely spoken. In tourist areas in the south Cyprus Tourism Organisation representatives can provide a degree of assistance. However, crime in Cyprus is at a reassuringly low level. Any problem is more likely to come from visitors. Take the usual precautions with regard to handbags and valuables left in cars. Any thefts or offences should be reported to the police, if only for insurance purposes.

- Do not cross the Green Line (the dividing line between the two sectors) except on a day trip from Nicosia south to the north.

- Keep away from military zones (north or south).

- Do not use roads marked as blocked-off on a map (they may encroach on military zones).

Police assistance:
☎ **112 (Republic)**
☎ **155 (North)**
from any call box

TELEPHONES

In the Republic public telephones are found in town centres. They take 2, 5, 10 and 20-cent coins or *telecards* (C£3, C£5, C£10, from banks, post offices, tourist offices or kiosks). In the north public phones are scarce. They take tokens (*jetons*) or *telekarts*, sold at Telekomünikasyon offices.

International Dialling Codes

From Cyprus to:

UK:	00 44	Germany:	00 49
USA:	00 1		
Netherlands:	00 31		
Spain:	00 34		

POST

Post Offices
There are main post offices in main towns and sub-post offices in the suburbs.
Republic Open: Mon–Fri 7:30–1:30 (Thu also 3–6)
Closed: Sat and Sun
North Open: Mon–Fri 8–1 and 2–5, Sat 8:30–12:30
Closed: Sun
☎ (02) 303219 (Republic)
☎ 2285982 (North)

ELECTRICITY

The power supply is: 240 volts

Type of socket: Square, taking three-square-pin plugs (as UK). In older buildings, round two-pin sockets taking two-round-pin (continental-style) plugs.

TIPS/GRATUITIES

Yes ✓ No ✗		
Restaurants (if service not included)	✓	10%
Cafés (if service not included)	✓	10%
Hotels (if service not included)	✓	10%
Hairdressers	✓	50p/£1
Taxis	✓	10%
Tour guides	✓	50p/£1
Cinema usherettes	✗	
Porters	✓	50p/bag
Cloakroom attendants	✓	50p
Toilets	✗	

PHOTOGRAPHY

What to photograph: landscapes, picturesque villages, bustling towns, flowers and wildlife.

Where it is forbidden to photograph: in both sectors near military camps or other military installations, in museums, and in churches with mural paintings and icons where flashlight is required.

Where to buy film: the most popular brands and types of film can be obtained from shops and photo laboratories. Film should not be bought from kiosks as it may well have been 'roasted'.

HEALTH

Insurance
Tourists get free emergency medical treatment; other services are paid for. For UK nationals benefits are available in the Republic by arrangement with the Department of Health before departure. Medical insurance is advised for all.

Dental Services
Dental treatment must be paid for by all visitors. Hotels can generally give recommendations for local dentists. Private medical insurance is strongly advised to all tourists to cover costs of dental treatment in Cyprus.

Sun Advice
Cyprus enjoys almost constant sunshine throughout the year. Wear a hat and drink plenty of fluids during the hot months (particularly July and August) to avoid the risk of sunstroke. A high-protection sunscreen is also recommended.

Drugs
Minor ailments can be dealt with at pharmacies (*farmakio* in the south, *eczane* in the north). Pharmacies sell all branded medicines. Some drugs available only on prescription in other countries are available over the counter in Cyprus.

Safe Water
Tap water in hotels, restaurants and public places is generally safe to drink though not very palatable in the north, particularly around Famagusta where the sea has invaded boreholes. Bottled water is cheap and widely available.

CONCESSIONS

Students Cyprus is not really on the backpacker's route. There is no such thing as a really cheap air fare and budget accommodation is limited. There are youth hostels in Nicosia, Larnaka, Pafos, Agía Napa and in the Troodos Mountains. For details contact: The Cyprus Youth Hostel Association, PO Box 1328, CY 1506 Nicosia (☎ 02-442027).

Senior Citizens Few concessions are made to elderly visitors. Most hotels offer discounts during the low tourist season, which for coastal resorts is mid-November to mid-March (excluding Christmas) but you do not have to be a senior citizen to take advantage.

CLOTHING SIZES

Cyprus/Europe	UK	USA	Rest of Europe	
46	36	36	46	Suits
48	38	38	48	Suits
50	40	40	50	Suits
52	42	42	52	Suits
54	44	44	54	Suits
56	46	46	56	Suits
41	7	8	41	Shoes
42	7.5	8.5	42	Shoes
43	8.5	9.5	43	Shoes
44	9.5	10.5	44	Shoes
45	10.5	11.5	45	Shoes
46	11	12	46	Shoes
36	14	14	36	Shirts
37	14.5	14.5	37	Shirts
38	15	15	38	Shirts
39/40	15.5	15.5	39/40	Shirts
41	16	16	41	Shirts
42	16.5	16.5	42	Shirts
43	17	17	43	Shirts
34	8	6	36	Dresses
36	10	8	38	Dresses
38	12	10	40	Dresses
40	14	12	42	Dresses
42	16	14	44	Dresses
44	18	16	46	Dresses
38	4.5	6	38	Shoes
38	5	6.5	38	Shoes
39	5.5	7	39	Shoes
39	6	7.5	39	Shoes
40	6.5	8	40	Shoes

WHEN DEPARTING

- Remember to contact the airport or airline 72 hours prior to leaving to ensure flight details are unchanged.
- Departure tax is included in the cost of an airline or ferry ticket in the southern Republic but in the north a tax of 1,000,000 Turkish lira is payable upon departure.
- Items of antiquity may not be taken out of Cyprus.

LANGUAGE

Cyprus has two official languages, Greek and Turkish. Greek is spoken in the Republic of Cyprus and Turkish in the north. Most Greek Cypriots speak good English but an attempt at the language is useful in for example the village coffee shop and similar places where locals may know no English. In the north things are different – not as much English is spoken. Waiters and others have only a limited fluency and some knowledge of Turkish is a definite advantage. Below is a list of some words that you may come across.

English	Greek	Turkish
hotel	*xenodhohío*	*otel*
room	*dhomátyo*	*oda*
...single/double	*monó/dhipló*	*tek/iki kishilik*
breakfast	*proinó*	*kahvalti*
toilet	*twaléta*	*tuvalet*
bath	*bányo*	*banyo*
shower	*doos*	*dus*
balcony	*balkóni*	*balkon*
bank	*trápeza*	*banka*
exchange office	*ghrafío sinalághmatos*	*kambiyo bürosu*
post office	*tahidhromío*	*postane*
money	*leftá*	*para*
cash desk	*tamío*	*kasa*
credit card	*pistotikí kárta*	*kredi karti*
traveller's cheque	*taxidhyotikí epitayí*	*seyahat çeki*
exchange rate	*isotimía*	*döviz kuru*
restaurant	*estiatório*	*restoran*
café	*kafenío*	*bar*
menu	*menóo*	*menü*
lunch	*yévma*	*ögle yemegi*
dinner	*dhípno*	*aksam yemegi*
dessert	*epidhórpyo*	*tatli*
waiter	*garsóni*	*garson*
the bill	*loghariazmós*	*hesap*
aeroplane	*aeropláno*	*uçak*
airport	*aerodhrómio*	*havaalani*
bus	*leoforío*	*octobüs*
...station	*stathmós*	*otogar*
boat	*karávi*	*gemi, vapur*
...port	*limáni*	*porto sarabi*
ticket	*isitírio*	*bilet*
...single/return	*apló metepistrofís*	*tek gidis/gidis dönüs*
yes	*ne*	*evet*
no	*óhi*	*hayir*
please	*parakaló*	*lütfen*
thank you	*efcharistó*	*tesekkür ederim*
hello	*yásas, yásoo*	*merhaba*
goodbye	*yásas, yásoo*	*hosça kal*
sorry	*signómi*	*özür dilerim*
how much?	*póso?*	*ne kadar?*
I (don't) understand	*(dhen) katalavéno*	*sizi anliyorum*

INDEX

Acknowledgements

The Automobile Association wishes to thank the following photographers, libraries and associations for their assistance in the preparation of this book.

HULTON GETTY 14; MARY EVANS PICTURE LIBRARY 10, 76b; MRI BANKERS' GUIDE TO FOREIGN CURRENCY 119; PA NEWS 11; SPECTRUM COLOUR LIBRARY F/Cover: old man, 57, 86

The remaining photographs are held in the Automobile Association's own picture library (AA PHOTO LIBRARY), with contributions from:
Malc Birkitt 5b, 7, 9b, 13, 19, 23, 26, 27a, 33, 34, 43, 45, 49b, 50, 54, 59, 60, 61, 68, 73, 76a, 78, 117a, 117b; Robert Bulmer 24, 25, 75, 80, 83; Alex Kouprianoff F/Cover: Cape Gkreko, B/Cover: wine bottle, 1, 2, 5a, 9a, 9c, 12, 15a, 15b, 16, 17, 18/19, 20, 21, 22, 28/9, 31, 35, 37, 38a, 38b, 39a, 48, 52, 56, 62, 64a, 65a, 67, 70, 72, 77, 79, 81, 87, 88, 90, 91a, 91b; Roy Rainford 6, 8b, 27b, 41, 44, 47, 49a, 58, 64b, 66; H Ulcan F/Cover: Soli Theatre, 85

Author's Acknowledgements

Robert Bulmer acknowledges the invaluable contribution of his daughter, Fiona Bulmer, in the preparation of this book. Thanks also to John Wood, General Manager of Le Meridien Hotel, Limassol for his generous assistance and to Holiday Autos International Ltd of Frimley, Surrey for arranging jeep hire.

Contributors
Copy editor: Penny Phenix Page Layout: Design 23 Verifier: David Hancock
Researcher (PracticalMatters): Colin Follett Indexer: Marie Lorimer

Dear Essential Traveller

Your comments, opinions and recommendations are very important to us. So please help us to improve our travel guides by taking a few minutes to complete this simple questionnaire.

You do not need a stamp (unless posted outside the UK). If you do not want to cut this page from your guide, then photocopy it or write your answers on a plain sheet of paper.

Send to: **The Editor, AA World Travel Guides, FREEPOST SCE 4598, Basingstoke RG21 4GY.**

Your recommendations...

We always encourage readers' recommendations for restaurants, nightlife or shopping – if your recommendation is used in the next edition of the guide, we will send you a *FREE* AA *Essential* Guide of your choice. Please state below the establishment name, location and your reasons for recommending it.

_____

_____

_____

_____

Please send me **AA *Essential*** _____

(see list of titles inside the front cover)

About this guide...

Which title did you buy?
  AA *Essential* _____
Where did you buy it? _____
When? m m / y y

Why did you choose an AA *Essential* Guide? _____

_____

_____

_____

_____

Did this guide meet your expectations?
  Exceeded ☐ Met all ☐ Met most ☐ Fell below ☐
  Please give your reasons _____

_____

_____

_____

continued on next page...

Were there any aspects of this guide that you particularly liked? _____

_____

_____

_____

Is there anything we could have done better? _____

_____

_____

_____

_____

About you...

Name (*Mr/Mrs/Ms*) _____

    Address _____

_____

_____ Postcode _____

    Daytime tel nos _____

Which age group are you in?

    Under 25 ☐ 25–34 ☐ 35–44 ☐ 45–54 ☐ 55–64 ☐ 65+ ☐

How many trips do you make a year?

    Less than one ☐ One ☐ Two ☐ Three or more ☐

Are you an AA member? Yes ☐ No ☐

About your trip...

When did you book? m m / y y   When did you travel? m m / y y

How long did you stay? _____

Was it for business or leisure? _____

Did you buy any other travel guides for your trip?

    If yes, which ones? _____

_____

Thank you for taking the time to complete this questionnaire. Please send
it to us as soon as possible, and remember, you do not need a stamp
(*unless posted outside the UK*).

Happy Holidays!